CONFUCIUS: In Life and Legend

Betty Kelen

CONFUCIUS
In Life and Legend

THOMAS NELSON INC.
Nashville   Camden   New York

Books by Betty Kelen:

A Children's Hour
Gautama Buddha

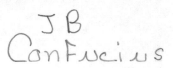

FOR RUBY COLLINS
in life-long friendship

Third Printing, February 1974

Copyright © 1971 by Betty Kelen

Library of Congress Catalog Card Number: 72–164970

International Standard Book Number: 0–8407–6152–X

MANUFACTURED IN THE UNITED STATES OF AMERICA

CONTENTS

The World of Confucius

Confucius is one of that handful of men whose name almost everybody in the world knows. Even small children, long before they meet the great Chinese sage in their school books, learn of a certain comic Confucius whose tipsy wisdom begins, "Confucius says . . ." The jest is usually far below the Master's standard, but it cannot diminish him; it only keeps alive the memory of his humanity and wit.

Confucius was an artist as well as a philosopher, and he had an artist's temperament—humility combined with immense self-esteem. If he could have looked down the track of time at his own history, we can suppose that he would have been gratified to know that his philosophy would shape the civilization of his people. The famous titles with which posterity honored him—the "uncrowned king of China" and the "Master and Model of Ten Thousand Generations"—might have irritated his simplicity-loving soul; but the thought of being immortalized in a fortune cookie would surely have provoked from him a smile.

Most of all it would have astonished him to realize that

hardly a man would ever walk the earth who was wiser than he.

"I am not wise by nature," he used to say. "I have become wise through hard work."

Such sturdy sayings, preserved for centuries, convey to us almost everything we know for certain about Confucius. From them we learn a great deal about the Master and the man—what sort of a person he was and what he thought about the world and others. But they contain hardly a hint of any circumstance or event that provides the framework of a factual biography. The series of disjointed happenings and anecdotes which, strung together, form the substance of the "life of Confucius" are remnants of memories and records first collected and written down by the court historian, Sse-Ma Ch'ien, 350 years after the Master's death. It is semi-legendary material, but that is not to say that truth is absent from it. Ancient chroniclers are not necessarily uncritical; and it is also possible that they had access to earlier sources now lost to us.

This book tells the story of Confucius as it has been known and cherished since ancient times, avoiding scholarly arguments except to point out where they might take place. Similar gaps and faults exist in our knowledge of all the great teachers of old. Often there are miracles to dazzle the mind so that we gladly suspend our judgment of fact. In the story of Confucius, there is no miracle, not one. He is only a sage lately fallen into a shadow, whom we shall lead forth to be examined by what meager light we have. Even so, he shines—a poor man who lived a rather desperate life, but he changed the world nevertheless.

The world Confucius knew flourished six hundred years before Christ, but he could look back upon a civilization ages old. In misty antiquity the race that was to call itself the black-haired people had begun to use a form of picture writing and had devised a system of counting. They had noted the useful life cycle of the silk-worm and had learned to reel silk from cocoons. In time, their tribes and clans settled compactly in the valley of the Huang Ho, the Yellow River, in northern China, drawing together in strong unity against the barbarian peoples that pressed them from round about.

There was a remote dynasty, the Hsia, which lasted until 1766 B.C. The Shang (or Yin) Dynasty followed. In very early times, chieftains and kings were elected, but in time kingship became hereditary, passing from father to son.

In 1122 B.C., the Chou kings came to power; this was the dynasty of Confucius. Centuries before he was born, when the power of the Chou was at its height, there was a Golden Age when the ingenuity and artistry of the black-haired people, which we admire to this very day, came to its first bloom. The silken clothing acquired subtle weaves and became heavy with glorious embroidery. There were bronze vessels of good workmanship and pottery smoothly made and decorated. Large and shapely buildings housed the well-to-do families, with pleasant gardens where ladies and gentlemen went walking, bowing and hissing at each other the polite syllable *tze,* which means "Master" or "Mistress."

The orderly march of heavenly bodies was noted and lunar and solar calendars were adjusted to it. There was music, and a means of writing down the notes. The early picture writing had developed into ideographs which could express not only things but thoughts. Poetry flourished. Recorded history had begun.

There was no god in the sense Westerners understand a god. However, there was Heaven, which consisted of a vast gathering of supernatural beings, including the souls of all the ancestors of the black-haired people, as well as elemental spirits, demons, and deities galore. The ghosts of ancestors usually lived in brightly painted temples at the bottom of the garden. Elemental spirits and demons inhabited natural holy places such as waterfalls, trees, or mountain shrines. Deities were everywhere, and all rolled up together they were "Heaven," which had a "will" and had to be placated with ritual and sacrifice, just as if it were a single person.

The kings of Chou built their capital city at Loyang (a town which is still on the map in the modern province of Honan), and they built other cities at choice sites in the river valley. They divided their land into states and districts, sending their brothers and sons to govern them from smaller towns and castles. These lesser rulers bore titles which we translate as "duke" or "prince." Their sons usually succeeded them in office.

Around such royal courts there gathered a hereditary

ruling class of lords and barons who owed the duke feudal allegiance. And below them on the social ladder was a hereditary landed gentry of knights and squires who were military men at heart, always on the lookout for an opportunity to seize power and make lords and barons —or even dukes—of themselves.

During the Chou Dynasty a widespread civil service was established, netting the realm together. It consisted of thousands of public offices filled by people of wealth and influence. By the time Confucius lived, these offices had become hereditary. When an officeholder died, his son filled the vacancy.

The black-haired people at large were goods-and-food suppliers to this weighty feudal and fat-cat super-structure. Usually they were artisans, farmers, herds-men, peasants, servants—in fact, they were serfs. As you might guess, it was hereditary to be a serf, also.

In the sixth century, when Confucius was born, the Chou rulers had long since passed their glory. The king was a useless figurehead and Loyang a city of cracked stones and broken bronze bells. The states were breaking away from central authority, and they frequently warred with one another. Within the lifetime of Confucius, social and political conditions degenerated swiftly. The years from 722 to 481 B.C. are called in history books by the pleasing name of "Spring and Autumn Period," but this is only a poetic way of stating a passage of time when things started out well, but became steadily worse.

And yet, looking back from our vantage point, we see clearly that the time of Confucius marked a victorious climax in the drama of humankind. Man had solved the physical problems of existence. He could clothe and feed himself, build shelter, take care of his health, even wring luxury out of his surroundings. Now, toward the end of the sixth century before Christ, and throughout the fifth century, there took place a great flowering of thought, a veritable wisdom explosion, and this happened in several widely separated areas of the world.

The great mystic Lao-tze, an older contemporary of Confucius who lived at Loyang, was looking inward toward the most hidden recesses of the mind. In India, Gautama Buddha was translating mystic insight into terms of worldly action. In the west, in Persia, Zoroaster taught; he saw such concepts as good and evil, right and wrong, acting in violent conflict on the world. In Italy, Pythagoras was wonder struck by the exact harmonies and balance of numbers. In Judea, the moral lessons of the last of the major prophets were being recorded with vehement and tragic force. In Greece, Socrates and his pupils tried to identify those purposes that live inside our minds and will not let us waste ourselves but prod us to think and act.

Confucius was one of these miraculous men who arose in the first morning light of history with a passion for grasping the nature of things. His mind bent itself on man the social animal and the demands made on individuals when they live in groups. Confucius was a political thinker.

The answer he brought to political problems was the same that wisdom always brings—morality. Man had to be moral in all his works. Politicians had to be fountainheads of morality so that the state would automatically function in a moral manner.

Of course, nobody listened to this extreme advice. Confucius, in his lifetime, was a failure. This was fortunate, because if he had not been, some prince would surely have caused him to be assassinated. Practical politicians, especially in turbulent times, would rather listen to common sense than to the truth.

But the truth endures. Once recognized and put into words, it has a way of entwining itself in human affairs, emerging little by little into concrete expression. Over the centuries, the ideals of Confucius have been reflected in the highest achievements of the Chinese people. Today, when our worldwide need to establish stable governments, and moral relationships between them, is urgently upon us, his voice reassures us in our striving. It can be done—indeed, it is in the nature of things that we should do it.

Man's ideals are not made up of dreams. They are castiron promises.

THE MAN

1. *"When I Was Young..."*

"When I was young, we were very poor..."

In growing up, some people comply with the conditions of their childhood; others defy them. Many great men have defied their origins. It is as if, in taking the leap away from their home ground, they have leaped higher than others. Thus, although Confucius was a great gentleman and a respecter of proper conduct, we should not be surprised to find that in the traditional story told of his birth, he was the illegitimate child of a teen-age girl and a man who was old enough to be her grandfather.

Shu-liang Ho, the father of Confucius, was seventy years old when his son was born. He was a retired soldier, the military commander of a rural district in the state of Lu, one of the smaller provinces in the domain of the Chou kings. He enjoyed something of a reputation in Lu. His name might well have survived in old tales, even if he had not been the father of such a remarkable son.

His family name was K'ung. It is recorded that his ancestry traced back to the illustrious K'ung family of the neighboring state of Sung, and some chroniclers even state that he was descended from the royal house. One of

17

the K'ungs of Sung had been a famous general; another was a philosopher who had founded a music school and library; and another was a high minister with a beautiful wife. A wicked prince cast his eyes upon this wife, and after that the K'ungs were forced to flee from their native state. They took refuge in Lu, where they had no property or influence. Their fortunes declined, and they became poor. In time, they acquired an asset—a giant boy, very ugly but of immense strength, who entered the service of the Duke of Lu as a mercenary soldier. This was none other than Shu-liang Ho; his feats of strength and courage were such that they were spoken about in the cottages of peasants and became part of the folklore of the land.

Once when Lu was at war with a neighboring state, Shu-liang Ho, at great personal risk helped the head of a mighty noble family, the Meng, to escape from his fortress by night, in disguise, through enemy lines. From that time forth the Meng family were his patrons—that is, they gave him employment and saw to it that he got on in the world.

Some years later an even more renowned adventure took place. The cluster of states that occupied the central portion of the valley of the Yellow River had formed an alliance against the restless barbarian tribes to the south. For defense purposes, they wished to establish a base at a certain fortified town, and they sent a military force, which included Shu-liang Ho, to occupy it.

However, the inhabitants of the town defended it with unexpected vigor and nimble strategy. Fighting valorously for a while, they suddenly flung open a gate to the besiegers, as if they wished to surrender. The troops of the central states rushed into the city, brandishing their swords victoriously in the air—until they heard the thud of the gate crashing down behind them. Trapped inside the hostile town, they turned in a panic and flung back against the stout wood, but it held, and the townsmen swarmed on them with swords, clubs, and boiling oil. Then the giant, Shu-liang Ho, grasped a section of the gate in his mighty hands, wrenched it from its hinge and wedged himself underneath. He held a space open until all his comrades could scramble through.

Obviously it was not only brute strength that distinguished Shu-liang Ho, but quick thinking, cool courage, and true feudal loyalty. The Duke of Lu rewarded him in his old age by placing him in military command of a small country district. Here he probably spent his time keeping villages in order and complaining to his cronies about his troubles at home. For this old soldier had a private tragedy—he had no sons. Although he had taken wife after wife, he was the father of girls and nothing but girls, excepting one boy, who was weak in body and perhaps in mind.

Feudal societies, which are armed societies, set small value on girls. They regard them as expensive luxuries needing to be installed in strong households guarded by armed men. In this imprisonment, efforts must be made to keep them perpetually occupied, entertained, and adorned, and this costs money.

Costly as women are to keep, they are even costlier to get rid of, and a man like Shu-liang Ho, with nine daughters—one more unattractive than the next if they resembled their father—was kept impoverished all his life by repeatedly having to lay forth money for their dowries. Nor could he look forward to a happier life after death, with no son to perform the sacrificial rites to his spirit, which would be doomed to wander in limbo, starving, envious of its fellow ghosts who every feast day ate themselves fat on the luscious offerings of their sons, grandsons, and great-grandsons.

And so, although there was certainly no excuse for this old soldier's having seduced a sixteen-year-old girl, there was at least a reason. Shu-liang Ho needed a son very badly. Failing to beget one inside his own household, he sought one outside it. He probably promised the young woman some reward or support, even marriage, if she bore him a proper son. According to a tradition, the young girl climbed the mountain called Ch'iu Ni—Mud Hill—to beg the mountain spirit to grant her the favor of a boy.

In 551 B.C., her wish was granted. In gratitude to the mountain spirit she gave the child the personal name of Ch'iu, which means "hill," and the public name Chung-Ni, which means something like "Mud's Younger Brother." He was a huge, ugly baby with a nose twisted all wrong and a dreadful bulge on his skull, a small replica of his father. Shu-liang Ho might have doted on him, but at this point he disappears from the scene of our story. Perhaps his wives locked him up. Two years later he died, and apparently the young mother was not invited to the funeral and perhaps not even told the burial place of her child's father. In any case, she did not pass this knowledge on to Confucius.

These events took place in the obscure village of Tsou.

Soon after the old man's death, the mother of Confucius took him to live closer to the state capital, Ch'ü-fu—a town which still flourishes as a modern city in southwestern Shantung.

Biographers of later times have bestowed a name upon the mother of Confucius, Cheng-tsai, and they have written that she belonged to the Yen clan. But it is hard to believe that a clan with solidarity and possessions would have given one of their young daughters to a very old man of no wealth, a state pensioner who would soon leave her a widow. We sense in the tradition that she belonged to the common people, the agricultural multitude who lived outside the walls of city and town—a peasant's daughter, a serf really. In the flat statement of one ancient biographer, she was "the daughter of the man Yen."

We don't know how this child-mother survived or supported her son. Knowing Confucius as we do, we can guess that she never let him forget, from earliest childhood, that he was not an ordinary poor boy but a knight's son and a descendant of the famous K'ungs of Sung.

It is said that a man who has been poor as a child will never get the chill of poverty out of his bones. Perhaps so, but Confucius' mother gave him the poor man's gifts of self-reliance and practicality. The Master hardly ever spoke about his youth, but he never denied his modest beginnings. "When I was young, we were very poor," he said. Then he added, possibly with a smile at his well-born pupils: "Perhaps that's why I can turn my hand to so many odd jobs."

2. *"When I Was Fifteen..."*

"When I was fifteen, I set my mind on learning."

We have no certain knowledge of how the young Confucius gained his education, or who his teacher was, or what he learned. We strongly sense in every one of his words that he was the sort of man who would have learned in any circumstances—from the university of life, from sensitive observation of nature, especially human nature, and that his mature opinions were founded on his ability to see into other people's minds. Once he gave to his pupils this advice: "At home respect your parents. Away from home respect your elders. Be honest; love man; love what is good. If you have time afterwards, study."

Study came last in his recipe of life. First came the human seasoning.

Yet he was one of the most studious men who ever lived, and many of his sayings show how well he loved the scholar's life. "Study as if you never could get enough of it," he said, "as if you were afraid something might get away from you."

This passionate love of books and learning was natural

to his mind, but it could not have developed so strongly unless someone had taken the trouble in his early years to teach him. He was only a poor woman's son, yet someone showed him how to recognize the complex, difficult ideographs; someone put into the boy's hands an ancient, clumsy book.

In the latter part of the Spring and Autumn Period, there was little political organization left in what remained the realm of the Chou kings. What there was, was feudal—that is, it had a military purpose. Each state was divided into districts and rural villages. The villages were grouped around noble families. The peasants who worked the land had feudal obligations and perhaps a sense of loyalty to the noble families who were supposed to protect them in time of war, and in fact owned them in war as well as in peace. As long as the villages and the communities of villages continued to feel secure under this arrangement, there was a feeling of solidarity. People took care of each other, and in this way the social system remained stable.

All this fell apart in the lifetime of Confucius. But when he was a boy, the benign breath of olden times was still in the air. It was the custom of the villages to support learned old men as teachers. Perhaps they might have been ancient clerks who had once served as stewards in rich houses. They spent their declining years training younger men for the same kind of post, so that every child in the area, regardless of his wealth or standing, had the right, if he had the will and ability, to acquire a certain amount of education. We are accustomed to hearing that the Chinese invented just about everything in the course of their long history, and sometimes it is said that they invented the public school also. It probably was in one of the first public schools in the world that Confucius learned his lessons. He may have paid the aged teacher as best his small means allowed, or not at all.

He must have learned, first of all, the "basics." These were not only reading, writing, and arithmetic, but the conciliation of spirits, both the evil ones that preyed on man and the benevolent ones that helped him. This was important knowledge for people who lived close to the terrors of early times, to the stunning crash of thunder, to the swift tragedy of flood and disease and the shuddering mystery of bewitched places. Rites had to be learned by heart; they involved incantations, gestures, and precise, humble sacrifice. They might be described as a system of etiquette betwixt man and Heaven, by means of which supernatural beings were kept friendly toward man.

Furthermore, there were the rules of behavior between men to learn, the polite manners and speech which are so important in a feudal society where everyone has his own proper place, either inherited from his father or bestowed upon him by his overlord. And there was such a thing as correct conduct between men and women, lord and vassal, knight and knight. These were rites too, but they had the regulatory effect of laws.

In those disordered times, with old ways crumbling everywhere, many people were beginning to think that etiquette was rubbish and ritual nothing but make-believe.

Certainly the princes, dukes, and high officials who were in charge of public ceremonies were slipshod in their duties. Mistresses, jewels, pompons of office were on their minds, not rituals, and they levied taxes and threw the people's money to the four winds.

Confucius, even when he was very young, showed signs that he was not slipshod. One of the earliest traditions of his boyhood relates that he loved to play at ceremonies. He had little sacrificial vessels, which he himself had perhaps modeled out of clay, and these he would set in correct array and move about with stately gestures, as grave as a priest at an altar.

He must have been an extremely noticeable boy. He grew while you looked at him; he was going to be a giant like his father. There was no doubt that he was extremely intelligent. Probably his mother realized this from the start, and in moving to a district close to the capital, she had meant to make it possible for him to obtain better schooling than he would have had in his native village of Tsou. He might even attract the attention of an important lord, who would give him a respectable post in the bureaucracy.

When he was still a very young man, perhaps only in his teens, his mother died.

Throughout his early years, so far as we know, Confucius had had no communications whatever with his father's family. Yet now he did a very purposeful thing. He had his mother temporarily buried, while he returned to the Tsou district to question people who might be able to point out to him his father's grave. An old woman told him that his father had been buried in Fang, a village where it is said Confucius' forebears had settled when they fled over the border from Sung.

He found the grave and reburied his mother next to his father.

This was a very grand gesture for such a young man, and a spectacular demonstration of the sort of person he was growing up to be. By this act, he proclaimed his ancestral roots, declaring to the world that he was not a common penniless orphan, but a gentleman of substantial family for whom the future should certainly contain an honorable place.

"The Superior Man's respect extends to all," he was to say. "It is at its greatest when he respects himself."

He claimed his father's name and rank; no doubt he performed the ancestral rites exactly as Shu-liang Ho would have wished, and continued to do so all his life. But that was all. He made no attempt to capitalize on the heroic reputation of his parent, and there is no evidence at all that he ever sought the patronage of his father's protectors, the Meng family.

Not one military skill did this soldier's son acquire, except archery, which everyone practiced as an everyday sport, nor had he any interest in military matters. It was his opinion that a moral person's first concern was peace, not war, and many years later, when a prince asked him to discourse on the military arts, he stiffly replied, "I know something about sacrifices and religious exercises, but I am quite ignorant of the doings of armies and troops."

3. "... my Accounts ..."

"It was only necessary that my accounts be correct."

In the years when Confucius was young, Duke Chao reigned in the state of Lu, but he was by no means the most important person in it. The real rulers were the Three Families, the Chi, the Meng, and the Shu. These were clans of powerful feudal landowners who divided almost all the land between them and controlled the public offices, jockeying and competing against one another in an intricate game of power politics. They had no objection to political murder, even to killing a duke or a minister, if it seemed in their interest.

During the time of Shu-liang Ho, the Meng had been the mightiest nobles in the land, but in the following years the Chi family, by means of a series of intrigues, had managed to draw most of the power to itself. By the time Confucius was fifteen years old, the Chi had gained control of the lion's share of the land, one half of the army, all the best positions at court—in fact, the Duke of Lu himself was their puppet.

It was this family that took note of the young Confucius and became his patrons, on and off, for a good part of his life. When he was young, perhaps still in his teens, he

was put to work in the accounting offices of one of the Chi
country estates—or rather in the granaries, since grain
was used for money. Later he was made overseer of their
flocks and grazing grounds. The fact that such a young
man was given a position of responsibility bears witness
to his outstanding abilities and the fact that they were
noticed and appreciated; still, these were hardly suitable
positions for a knight's son and a descendant of the
K'ungs of Sung. What Confucius longed for, and thought
he deserved to get, was some far more sophisticated post
in the city which would lead him eventually to a dignified
office in which, when he reached a proper age, he would
be entrusted with important duties of administration and
the performance of state and religious ceremonies.

He seems to have had the opportunity, early in his life,
to visit the state capital, the present-day Ch'ü-fu, where he
became acquainted with those books we now know as
the *Classics*. These were already centuries old when Confucius was born. They were inscribed with a stylus on
slats of wood, bound together with thongs of leather in
the manner of Venetian blinds. Such books were durable,
to say the least, but they were not easy to carry about,
and they were usually kept in archives in capitals and
fortresses. Since we cannot imagine that there were
many such books in the country places where Confucius
counted herds and kept accounts, we must imagine that
he had occasion, perhaps while rendering his accounts to
his superiors, to visit Ch'ü-fu quite often.

One of the *Classics* was the *I Ching*, or *Book of Changes*,
a strange work consisting of a collection of sixty-four

different patterns, each composed of six horizontal lines, solid or broken, and of the same length, so that when they were arranged one under the other, they formed a square.

Perhaps originally these lines represented magic sticks or wands, or perhaps divining bones that a priest threw on the ground for the purpose of reading the future in the patterns they made. As collected in the *I Ching,* each of the sixty-four possible combinations had come to have a meaning or a series of meanings handed down since remotest antiquity. To this day, those who are fond of occult mystery find endless fascination in this ancient book. Confucius was not of a mystical turn of mind, and in his youth he did not interest himself greatly in the *Changes;* and yet, when he was old, it is said that he became engrossed in them.

From the beginning, however, he fell in love with the *Book of Odes,* the *Shih Ching.* Possibly the collection of folk songs, anthems, and hymns that we know today under the same name is not unlike the one Confucius read and, in the course of his life, edited, sifted, and added to.

The oldest poems must have been scraps of thought passed down from man's most ancient beginnings; the main part dated from the beginning of the Chou Dynasty, from the days of the heros, King Wen and King Wu. At first reading, it is hard for us to understand the very great reverence Confucius had for the *Odes,* and what it was about them that caused him to say, "He who has not studied them is standing with his face against a stone wall." The poems are charming and have a gentle grace reminiscent of pre-Elizabethan songs and ballads, but they do not seem to possess great intellectual power.

If grand inspiration has been drawn from the *Odes,* and if their lyric beauty has penetrated every form of Chinese art, ancient and modern, it is because for centuries, long before Confucius, these old folk songs were thought to contain primeval wisdom, handed to man by Heaven. Like the tales of the Old Testament, they were divine messages, couched in symbolic language, and their imagery could be applied to any sort of human, social, or political situation.

For Confucius, bored among his sacks of grain and herds of livestock, the *Odes* were a springboard into the realms of thought. By the time he was old he knew more about their interpretation than any man alive. In his youth we may imagine him on his visits to Ch'ü-fu, sitting in dim corridors, listening to the exercises of the blind court musicians who knew them all by heart. He was himself a natural musician, and he could usually master anything in the way of singing or instrumentation that he set out to learn. He practiced singing or chanting the *Odes* rhythmically, in formal syllables, careful to pronounce them—and all speech—in the best accent of his time.

One day he requested the Music Master of Lu to teach him to play the zither. For ten days this gentleman allowed his ears to be affrighted by the noises Confucius was producing from his instrument, and finally he said, "Well, well, you've practiced enough. We had better try something else."

"No," said Confucius. "I have learned the melody now —it is the rhythm that escapes me." Earnestly he twanged away. After some time longer, the Music Master said, "Now you have practiced the rhythm, let's go on to something else."

"No," said Confucius. "I haven't quite caught the mood." Relentlessly he continued to play until the Music Master said, with impatience, "Now you have practiced the mood, let us proceed."

"No," said Confucius. "I haven't yet sensed the man who wrote the music."

Now the Music Master began to open his ears to this strangely persistent pupil, and he noted how deftly the huge fingers were moving, drawing a range of emotions from the instrument. He listened and from time to time spoke: "Now you seem serious and thoughtful. . . . Now you are cheerful and your hopes are high."

Suddenly Confucius stopped playing, his face alight. "Now I know who he was. He was a dark man, swarthy, and tall—oh, he must have been a great, tall man. His eyes were like those of a ram looking into the distance, and his mind was like a King of the Four Quarters of Heaven. Who but King Wen could have composed this music?"

The Music Master arose from his mat in astonishment, and he bowed twice, with awe, to his young pupil, saying with awe, "You have guessed correctly. Among us musicians there is a tradition that the composer of this music was King Wen."

Confucius made friends with these learned blind

men, and he always remembered their teaching with gratitude. Even when he became a venerable sage at the courts of princes, he used to astonish everyone by giving up his seat to a blind musician, even to much younger men with no rank whatsoever.

"I love old things," said Confucius, "and I love to dig them out." As ardently as he practiced the *Odes,* he searched the *Book of History,* the *Shu Ching,* which related the words and deeds of the old hero-kings of Chou. Foremost among these were the founders of the dynasty, King Wu and his musical brother, King Wen. Just as old buildings are covered by ivy, which obscures their cracks and leaves only the light of their windows to shine forth, the faults of these legendary monarchs had become shrouded by time, and only their virtues endured, glowing through the mysterious centuries.

Greater even than the ancestor kings in the eyes of Confucius was King Wen's son, the Duke of Chou. It was this prince who, leading an army eastward from his father's domain, had founded the state of Lu. What is more, there were some who said that he was the actual author of the *History* and the original collector of the beloved *Odes* and composer of their music—a lofty-minded and artistic prince who was the natural focus of the idealism of the young Confucius. And it is likely that, when Confucius came to the capital, he loved nothing better than to lose himself in a library containing the literature in which he could read about his hero, and in his secret imagination could transform himself into a modern counterpart of the illustrious Duke of Chou.

There was every reason for Confucius to bury himself in dim corridors when he visited Ch'ü-fu. If his mother, gazing at her peculiar-looking son, had ever trembled for fear of what he was going to look like when he became a man, those fears were justified. He was huge and ugly. One ancient account says that he was nine feet six inches tall. Even granting that the Chou foot-measure was somewhat shorter than ours, this still makes him about seven feet tall. His unevenly shaped head had not become smoother with growth. His wide-set eyes were wide open and staring in a manner that the black-haired people do not admire to this day. His nose, on which grew warts, was a lump twisted askew, unpleasantly high at the ridge. His upper teeth were so prominent that the two great front ones splayed out and overlay his bottom lip, even when his face was in repose.

In the years of his prime, kindness and equable humor mantled these unattractive features and made them pleasant, but when he was young he was unsightly, and probably awkward and gauche. Therefore he shrank out of sight and acquired the habit of shyness, and his friends, besides the blind musicians, were the Duke's historians and chroniclers. As he fell deeply in love with learning, he spent long hours questioning them, and also the temple officials, priests, antiquarians, curators, and artists —all who cared not a jot what a boy looked like so long as he was blessed with those wonderful scholarly gifts: a magpie's eye, a monkey's curiosity, and a memory like a bear trap.

At a young age he married. We do not know the

name of his wife or anything about her. Not one word is recorded, except that she bore Confucius a son and a daughter. It is possible that at the time the son was born, Confucius occupied a minor post in the civil service, since Duke Chao, to celebrate the event, sent him a carp. It was just about the most insignificant gift that a ruler could give anyone, but out of tact or gratitude, Confucius named the child First Carp, no doubt hoping to become the father of a procession of younger carps. But he had no other sons.

It is believed that Confucius did not live with his wife very long, but we do not know if they separated or if he became a widower.

4. *"At Thirty . . ."*

"At thirty, I could stand on my own feet."

The unsettled youth of Confucius, spent between city and country, court and countinghouse, musty libraries and golden pastures, gave him familiarity with many different classes of men and with their problems and discontents, which were increasing year by year. He identified the symptoms—society's moral fiber was wearing thin. And he recognized the reason—people were afraid. Rebellions were beginning to break out on the estates. Squabbles between states were an ever-present danger. Wars were in the air, and the rulers could not be trusted to avoid them.

Confucius observed that things had been different in the Golden Age when his hero, the Duke of Chou, had lived. Then rulers had been virtuous, and through them virtue had infused the land.

He began to ask himself, What was this magical quality of virtue that brought peace and prosperity wherever it reigned? He saw it as an attribute of Heaven which was reflected in the many-faceted world of men. It was mirrored, first of all, in the stately rhythms of Nature. It was evident in the order of poetry and music. Where

35

order lived, there lived virtue. Order was obviously the lost ingredient that had to be restored to society and politics.

And so he tirelessly questioned old priests and officials, trying to recapture ancient order. He did not, like some, see state rituals as mere spectacles or patriotic gestures. They were the poetry of state, the music of politics. If he could ascertain exactly how they had been performed in the Golden Age, and could perform them thus again, society would once more dance to their splendid notes.

Confucius was not the only person of his times who was trying to gather in the strength of the past with which to bolster the tottering realm. In a neighboring state, an eminent prime minister had recently codified the laws and cast them in bronze—and he had done this at the risk of displeasing mighty nobles who preferred to make up their own laws. Again, in the state of Ch'i, to the north, another official had written a treatise on political science, a work which Confucius had probably read. The sheer wastefulness of the crumbling society was calling forth codifiers, consolidators, formulators—people who were trying to preserve their institutions and customs by writing them down.

Confucius was influenced by such men, but his thought went beyond conventional law and dealt directly with the substance of law—human nature. One day he was to say, "If you use laws to direct people and punishments to control them, they will only evade the laws and develop no conscience. But if you guide them by virtue and control them by customs, they will have a conscience and a sense of what is right."

In his youth he had set himself to study. In his late twenties, he was one of the best-educated men of his time. Yet in spite of his qualities, he had not been offered the respectable position he craved as a functionary of state. Even naming his son after the Duke's carp had not gained him further favor, and his patrons, the Chi family, failed to grant him one of the numerous offices that were in their power to confer.

We can't tell why. His utter lack of money and influence was of course the main hindrance. Apart from that, anyone who studies closely the fragmentary story of Confucius' life cannot help suspecting that the father of Chinese etiquette was not necessarily the most tactful man in the world. He was far too outspoken—and blunt-spoken too. In his younger years he was probably something of a country bumpkin. A curious story has survived that once, when he was young, even still in mourning for his mother, he tried to crash a dinner party held by the Lord of Chi for officials of state. The steward of the Chi, Yang Hu, rebuffed him in cruel terms: "My lord has invited everyone of importance. He has not the honor of inviting you."

Knowing the mighty pride of Confucius, we realize how such an episode must have crushed him. Much later, when he became a master of etiquette, he was always careful to spare the feelings of the young and uninstructed.

No doubt he continued to hold some slight office, not one that added luster to the name of the K'ungs of Sung or gave him the opportunity to put his ideas of government into practice or to put the rituals right. As the years of his youth passed and he was overlooked, he bemoaned his fate, not yet perceiving how wisdom is engendered by misfortune. One day he was to teach his pupils: "Do not worry about not having a high position. Worry about filling the one you have got."

And he said, "Don't worry about who knows you. Just make sure you are worth knowing."

It seems certain that by the time he was thirty he had begun to impart some of his knowledge to others—that is, to teach. His pupils were young men of his own age who hoped to get posts in government, but unlike himself had not the patience or self-discipline to educate themselves. They might well have been the sons of knights. That in-between military class was becoming restless about this time, finding that it ought to have much more money, power, palaces, and positions at court than it had, and was determined to get them by working up the bureaucratic pyramid, or else by rebellion.

Probably these pupils contributed to the livelihood of Confucius. After his first youth, we hear no more of dull work in country countinghouses. Apparently he lived in the city like other people of the gentler classes.

Some public attention probably came his way when the old head of the house of Meng died. This was probably his father's old patron, but it was not of the valiant soldier, Shu-liang Ho, that the aged nobleman found himself thinking on his deathbed, but of a more remote forebear, one of the famous K'ungs of Sung, the philosopher who had founded a music school. The dying Lord of Meng had a presentiment that Confucius, like his distinguished ancestor, was going to do something with his life. He therefore called his heirs to him and said, "I have heard that the descendants of philosophers, even though they have no honor in their own times, eventually become famous. Just now K'ung Ch'iu is young, but he has a serious mind, and perhaps he will be great. Promise me that when I am dead, you will take him as your teacher."

In this way the heirs of the mighty Meng family joined the company of Confucius' pupils, and we may be sure that wherever they went, other young nobles came fastened to their heels like shadows.

As time went by, the young man K'ung Ch'iu or, as it was proper to call him, K'ung Chung-Ni (the Younger Brother of Mud), was more often called Master K'ung —or, to put it correctly, K'ung Fu-tze.

And to put it incorrectly, as the Jesuit fathers did, who first tried to spell these explosive syllables: Confucius.

5. "At Forty ..."

"At forty I knew exactly what I was about."

In 517 B.C., when Confucius was thirty-four years old, an episode occurred which might illuminate for us the reason why none of the great and powerful lords who ruled the state of Lu, using Duke Chao as their tool, saw fit to offer Master K'ung a post in government. In that year, on the anniversary when the people of Lu customarily held celebrations in honor of their ancestors, Duke Chao celebrated the rites at his family temple, invoking the spirits of his noble dead—the Duke of Chou and all the ancient heroes and princes of the royal line. These were the state ancestors of Lu.

This ought to have been a gorgeous occasion, with crowds of onlookers thronging the courts. As it was, so little respect did the state ceremonies command that the Duke's family temple had long fallen into neglect and poverty. Only two dancers could be mustered, and the voices of a few old musicians fluttered on the air like tattered ribbons.

Quite different was the scene at the family temple of the mighty head of the Chi family, Baron P'ing. Here the brightly painted red and golden walls trembled with the

40

sound of tambour and drum, and in the courtyard, which was crowded with townspeople, eight rows of dancers stamped upon the ground, each row numbering eight, swaying and rocking in their shining silken garments, forming and re-forming their groups. The fact that Baron P'ing was his patron did not persuade Confucius to hold his tongue at this bold rivalry with the royal house. "Eight rows of dancers!" he exclaimed. "Eight dancers to each and every row! A man who is not ashamed of this display is absolutely shameless!"

Baron P'ing heard and refrained from chopping off Master K'ung's head, but he did not feel obliged to pour honors on it either.

Not long after, the Duke and the Lord of Chi had another difference of even more serious nature. We do not know the details, but it concerned a cockfight. Bets were possibly the point at issue, or poisoned birds. Whatever it may have been, it was the last straw in the unfriendly relations that existed between the ducal throne and the house of Chi.

In 517 B.C., the very year that Baron P'ing had so ostentatiously honored his ancestors, one of his vassal knights rose up in rebellion and succeeded in imprisoning the Baron in a fortress to which he then laid siege. In vain did Baron P'ing offer bribes and inducements. The rebel refused to lift the siege, because he had the support of none other than Duke Chao, who had collected bits and scraps of an army around him with which he thought he could ruin the Lord of Chi, after which he intended to ruin the Meng and the Shu also.

However, the Lords of Meng and Shu saw through this plan. Perceiving that their best interests lay in preserving the established order, they swiftly sent to the aid of their distressed colleague of Chi troops which tore into Duke Chao's armies, scattering them to the winds.

The Duke fled northward for his life, taking refuge in the neighboring state of Ch'i.

Throughout this turmoil, Confucius found himself on the horns of a dilemma, not knowing exactly where his loyalties lay—with the Lord of Chi who provided him with bread and butter, or with the sorry, silly, cockfighting descendant of his beloved hero, the Duke of Chou.

Of course, he followed the Duke into exile. This sense of loyalty to the central authority, going over the heads of feudal overlords, became a cornerstone of his thinking. In the years to come it was to foster the unity of all China, but for the time being it was quite at variance with the narrower feudalism of his times, even of the Master's closest friends and disciples, who considered him quite radical in this respect.

Confucius could not possibly expect his impoverished Duke to support him in Ch'i, and so he took service with a certain nobleman, hoping that his presence would become known to the ruler of Ch'i, Duke Ching, who would then offer him a post in government.

Duke Ching did hear of him. One suspects that Master K'ung, in his forties, was not an easy man to overlook. The awkwardness of his youth was overcome; pride had taught him to carry his huge bulk with ponderous elegance. In company, he was interested in people and their doings, and he was full of information about how things had been done in the past and might be done in the future. His knowledge of the rites and traditions—we would say "the law"—was limitless. He was impressive, charming, and brilliant.

However, he was not talkative. He was too shy for that, and in fact he had a lifelong distaste for wordy people. "Words should cover what you want to say and stop right there," Confucius said. He spoke simply and crisply, so that people remembered what he said and repeated his observations, and since they were brief, they often seemed to be the soul of wit.

Duke Ching summoned this interesting exile to audience, and he put to him a question: What, in Master K'ung's view, was the secret of successful government?

Confucius replied in his spare style: "Let the prince be a prince. Let the servant be a servant. Let the father be a father, and the son a son."

Duke Ching, like a good Chinese, was quick at discerning symbolic meanings, and he read between the lines of these strange words. Good government, in the opinion of Master K'ung, hinged upon creating a stable society in which words meant exactly what they said. A prince had to be a prince with all the virtuous and noble qualities suggested by the word "prince." He should not, for example, be a cockfighting nincompoop. A servant was to be a servant, not a secret enemy or rebel. Unless fathers were worthy of that august name, setting a good example to their sons, who would then grow up in a spirit of filial devotion, the times would be out of joint.

The state was like a lute from which harmony was struck —if humans were not in correct relation to one another, it would produce only discord.

The second time Duke Ching called Confucius to an audience, he again asked him, "What is the secret of good government?" Confucius replied, "Good government consists in being sparing with resources."

These responses pleased Duke Ching very much. The idea germinated in his mind that he had found the very man to govern a large portion of his land. "I can't settle on you such fiefs as are held by your noble Chi family," he said apologetically to Confucius. "I can only give you something between the Chi and the Meng."

This promise set Confucius walking about in a golden haze of happiness. Here, in a foreign state, he had achieved the rewards which had been denied him at home. It was not, of course, the mere possession of land that rejoiced him. Confucius was not a greedy man. However, he was ambitious, and he thought in grandiose terms. He could hardly wait to take possession of this huge estate and turn it upside down in order to use it as a clean crucible in which to try out his ideas of good government.

But before this dream of his life could come true, a certain minister got to the ear of Duke Ching. He was not an enemy of Confucius, just a practical politician who did not believe that government was safe in the hands of idealists.

"Scholars!" he said to the Duke. "You know how they are. They are good talkers but conceited. They don't get

on well with the common people. They know all about
how to put together a magnificent funeral, what mourning
dress to wear, the size of the coffin, and how to sing the
dirge—but what do they know about everyday behavior?

"Look at this Master K'ung. Always making rules for
coming and going, bowing and walking! Rules! He's got
enough to last a thousand lifetimes. But what have these
rules to do with *ruling?*"

Duke Ching evidently decided in favor of his minister;
he did not bestow fiefs upon Confucius.

In spite of his disappointment, in later years Confucius
used to remember his exile in Ch'i with deep, tender
nostalgia. In that state had been preserved an old and
stately mode of music, so lovely to his ears that when he
first heard it, he exclaimed, "I never would have believed
the beauty of music could reach such polish!"

He went to the music school to hear the orchestral
music of Ch'i, and learned for the first time what true
virtuosity was and how well Heaven's harmonies found
expression through the minds and hands of men dedicated
to achieving perfection. For the seven years he remained
in exile, he placed himself as a pupil in the hands of the
Music Master of Ch'i, and for the first three months, we
are told, so immersed was he in music that "he forgot
the taste of meat."

6. *"Riches and Honors"*

"Riches and honors unrighteously won—
these are to me but a floating cloud . . ."

There are certain episodes in the traditional life-story of Confucius which seem to be less a chronicle of events as attempts by his admirers of a much later date to explain why public office was never conferred upon him. The Ch'i fiasco is a case in point. It is altogether unlikely that in his lifetime Confucius maddened people by wanting to impose on them all sorts of trivial rules of etiquette; he was a man who advised moderation and restraint in all things. But the later Confucians (who did so madden people) felt that explanations were in order, and so they supplied them.

We too wonder at the Master's dismal failures. We gain the strong impression from the story that Confucius, like many geniuses, had to suffer the penalty of being a queer duck: being left out of things. In the *Book of History* we read the statement: "If one is a good son and a good brother—that is being in government." This became a cornerstone of the Confucian doctrine—that a well-run state is the result of the harmonious interaction of all its parts, even the smallest part. On this foundation

46

the Chinese family system remained stable for many centuries.

Yet, it might have begun as the rather lame response of the Master to inconsiderate people who asked him why he had no official post. To intimate friends he did not hesitate to utter his nagging sense of disappointment: "I give the best that is in me—still I am not permitted to put it at the service of the state."

His misfortunes prompted him to pose questions of man's personal worth. Were "losers" who failed to climb the bureaucratic pyramid inferior to those who pushed ahead? Certainly not; but the injustice must be counterbalanced by self-cultivation. "A Superior Man complains about his shortcomings, not that others do not notice his qualities."

Even poverty, which Confucius had felt on his own skin, in itself had no power to degrade. "A Superior Man can be reduced to extremity; an ordinary man can be reduced to nonentity."

A man's measure dwelt not outside but inside him, and it was under his control.

Guided by acute observation and inspired by his hero, the Duke of Chou, whose thoughts he found recorded in the ancient books, he defined the Superior Man in terms that are recognizable, and also useful, the world over and at all times. So far as he was capable, he strove to personify his ideal, bearing misfortune with dignity and holding no grudge against any man, though sometimes he did not forbid himself a robust protest against sheer bad luck.

The years of his prime were spent in Ch'i, but he remained deeply attached to his homeland. "Only a bit of a change," he told his friends in Ch'i, "would make Lu perfect. And only a bit of a change would make Ch'i like Lu."

Meanwhile, the government of Lu was firmly in the hands of the Three Families, with Baron P'ing holding the reins. Such was his insolence that he dared to wear the ornamental jewel of office which rightfully belonged to the exiled Duke.

For seven years the Duke remained in exile. Then, about 509 B.C., he paid a visit to a little town on the border between Lu and Ch'i. Perhaps he had gone there in the hope of negotiating with emissaries of the Three Families for his restoration to the throne. We shall never know, because he died then and there, most opportunely for his enemies and probably by poison. However, after his death, his younger brother, Ting, was permitted to return to Lu as Duke, and with him went all the loyal exiles, including Confucius.

And now it seemed that the mysterious "changes" that guide men's lives had been recast into a fortunate pattern for Confucius. It had done his reputation no harm to be known as a man of uncompromising loyalty to his Duke in misfortune. Moreover, his knowledge of ancient ceremonials and court etiquette was gaining respect, and his wise sayings about government were being repeated in high councils of state. Back in Ch'ü-fu, his old pupils swiftly gathered around him, and new ones came, even from distant places, hoping to acquire from him the polish and learning that would allow them to perform worthily the rites and duties of dignified positions. It might have dawned on him then that he was cut out by Heaven to be a teacher rather than a public official—but at that point dazzling offers of public office suddenly began to shower upon him.

This change of fortune came about as the result of another severe political shake-up. This time it was the result of the intrigues of a sinister rebel whose ambition it was to govern Lu without the help of polish, learning, rites, etiquette, or anything at all except a strong arm and a bloody sword. His name was Yang Hu, and he was a steward of the house of Chi. He came to power by means of a shrewd trick.

Not long after the restoration of the ducal crown, Baron P'ing, the Lord of Chi, died. Even before the old rascal was in his grave, squabbles broke out among his vassals and family members about the funeral rites. Ought the Baron to be buried with his ill-gotten ornamental jewel of office or without it? Yang Hu cleverly whipped up this argument into a full-scale family quarrel, and when it was raging hot enough, he sprang into the breach, pretending to be a peacemaker. He captured P'ing's heir, Baron Huan, marched him into the public square in front of the Southern Gate of Ch'ü-fu, and there, before all the citizens, he made him swear certain oaths, expelling his most powerful friends and relations from Lu, and concentrating the authority of the Chi family in the hands of his faithful steward, Yang Hu.

With the most powerful men of Chi thus subdued, Yang Hu now terrorized the Meng and the Shu into similar obedience. By a series of bold moves, he made himself dictator of Lu; and he held the little state in the hollow of his hand. Far from wasting the jewel of office on the corpse of Baron P'ing, he wore it himself, and forcing from office all who might have opposed him, he looked around for new and untried officials to run his government.

He summoned Confucius to audience. Confucius refused the invitation. His soul loathed this bandit, the very man who years before, when Confucius was young and crude, had sneered at his clumsy attempt to attend a dinner party given by the Lord of Chi.

Yang Hu swallowed the insult and sent Confucius the present of a fat suckling pig. This obliged Confucius to pay Yang Hu a visit of thanks. But he was careful to pay it when he was sure that the dictator was not at home.

Yang Hu now let it be widely known that he intended to offer Confucius high public office. Again the Master was caught between self-interest and principle. Of course, such dilemmas are familiar to everyone, and most people try to think of a way to have their cake and eat it too. But easy solutions are not for philosophers, to whom the moral proposition is always blazingly clear. When there was a choice of loyalty between his Duke and the Chi, Confucius had chosen to follow the Duke into exile, but when he had to choose between the Chi and a swaggering bully, he sided with the fallen house of Chi.

And yet, it was not merely loyalty to his former protectors that made him rebuff Yang Hu. Who were the Chi family, after all? Only the descendants of bullies whose forebears had bent fortune to their will as forcefully as Yang Hu. According to the rites and traditions, all the authority of Lu was vested in the person of young Duke Ting, the descendant of that ancient hero, the Duke of Chou, who in the eyes of Confucius had made the very earth virtuous by walking on it. It was to the young Duke that the Master was loyal, and beyond him to the King, the head of the dynasty, in Loyang, and beyond them both to a historic heritage of strength, morality, virtue, and beneficent government. Now and forever, a primeval ideal of government filled the Master's mind, and it was to this he gave his total loyalty.

The fragmentary anecdotes that survive of this period under the dictatorship show us Confucius, an artistic and creative thinker, standing apart from his society like an artist from his painting, seeing its faults and passionately desiring to change them—and yet, like a fine artist, refusing to place a stroke that was not exactly right.

Yang Hu persisted in his efforts to bring Confucius into his government; he was shrewd enough to realize his worth. He created an occasion for meeting Confucius on the street. Like Confucius himself, he was a giant. He placed his monolithic strength in front of the huge philosopher and said abruptly, "I want a word with you."

Confucius paused.

"Do you consider it an act of your so-called Superior Man," inquired Yang Hu, "to own a priceless jewel and cheat the state of it?"

He was referring to the knowledge and genius of Confucius, and Confucius, though perfectly aware of the crass flattery, could only reply with a stiff "No."

Yang Hu pursued his advantage: "And do you call the man wise who, in spite of wanting to serve his state, continually lets slip his chances and ducks out of the way?"

To which Confucius, perhaps not without bitterness, could again reply only "No."

"Time is flying," said Yang Hu. "The years won't stand still for us!"

To which Confucius, to the very great shock of his admirers for centuries to come, replied, "Very well. I accept public office."

The sudden capitulation to the dictator's whim is hard to explain. Perhaps for a moment Confucius could not resist the tempting future dangled before him, or it might have occurred to him that Yang Hu, bully and giant, would have found it easy to draw his dagger and kill him on the spot.

The important fact is that, although the anecdote shows him giving in, in fact he never took office under Yang Hu. It is possible that time and again he had to wriggle out of similar tricky encounters. He wished to transform Lu radically, but not with a scoundrel directing his hand.

Another episode, closely entwined, shows the direction of his thoughts. At the same time that Yang Hu had leaped to power, another vassal of the Chi, in another part of the land, had seized his opportunity to make himself the master of a fortified city and the territory round about. He let it be known that he would be delighted to make Confucius the prime minister of these lands.

Confucius did not have the same animosity to this rebel as to Yang Hu. He was strongly tempted to join the rebellion. He was dissuaded by his disciple and best friend, the conventional, feudal-minded Tze Lu, who thought that the Master had gone mad to trifle with feudal loyalties in this way.

"Oh, can't I break free? Is everything to be in vain?" cried Confucius to Tze Lu. Then he added the words that betray his true aim and high ambition: "If only I could join him, I might build up again the kingdom of the Chou."

The reign of Yang Hu was brought to an end in quite a dramatic fashion. The dictator had decided that his puppet, Baron Huan, the heir of the house of Chi, should die, and he made elaborate arrangements to assassinate him. In the most courteous manner possible, he invited the Baron to perform an important sacrifice of state in the public square, and on the great day, he caused all the war chariots of Lu to be assembled there, elegantly displayed in rows, and handy for controlling the crowds in case they should protest the bloody deed.

He sent the state carriage, brilliant with new ribbons, to convey Baron Huan to the square. But somehow word of the fate in store for him had come to the ears of the Lord of Meng, and he had contrived to put Huan on his guard. Huan mounted the state carriage, but he managed to persuade or bribe the coachman to take a wrong turn and pull up in front of the town residence of the Meng family. There he sprang to the ground and slipped to safety in a door left open for him.

At that moment, in the street, some warriors in the pay of the Meng began to riot and incite the citizens to riot. The fracas spread from street to street, throughout the town of Ch'ü-fu; possibly Yang Hu did not find it useful to have his war chariots bottlenecked in the public square.

In the end his government fell, and the giant dictator took to his heels across the northern border, toward the hospitable home of Lu's discarded rulers, the state of Ch'i.

7. *"To Be a Prince..."*

"To be a prince is difficult;
to be a minister is far from easy."

Now the luck of Confucius shifted again, and this time the fateful "changes" fell in a dazzling pattern. Thanks to Tze Lu's excellent advice, he had emerged from the recent troubles with a spotless reputation as a man of fine feudal loyalty. What is more, the person who at that moment stood in need of loyalty was the one man to whom Confucius could be, in good conscience, impregnably loyal—Duke Ting of Lu.

This harassed ruler had not had a moment's peace since he ascended the throne, having been pulled back and forth like a puppet by one usurping power or another. Now he found himself in a more focal position than he had formerly occupied. The rebel Yang Hu had stirred up internal discord within the Three Families, so that they did not immediately regain their solidarity and power. Destiny was looking straight at Duke Ting, and Ting was looking around for someone to lean on. It was the hour of Confucius.

In the year 501 B.C., when he was just fifty years old, according to the chronicles Confucius was given his first public office of any importance—that of governor of the middle district of Lu.

How well he might have ruled, we may judge by reading some of his preserved words: "Maldistribution is a greater evil than scarce resources." And he said also, "Insecurity is a greater evil than poverty." Not until modern times would statesmen see so clearly that the livelihood of people was the secret core of history.

In due course the Duke called him further into the heart of government, raising him to the highest cabinet rank as Minister of Public Works, an office which he also discharged with credit. He then became the Minister of Justice, and it is recorded that during his tenure of office there was a sharp reduction of wrongdoing in the state of Lu.

A number of sayings suggest that he applied some thought to the subject of crime and punishment. Unlike modern sociologists, he did not blame crime on poverty but on unbridled affluence. He observed that families which for several generations had enjoyed comfort without self-discipline seldom respected orderly rules. And he recalled also from the *Book of History* a remark of the Duke of Chou: "Among the ordinary people, the parents labor to sow and reap, but their sons do not understand hard work. They lounge in the streets, vulgar in speech, disorderly in behavior."

We have no preserved tradition about Confucius as a judge, only his modest judgment of himself: "Another can judge a case as well as I. What I would like to do is correct the conditions that bring cases about."

As time passed, Confucius became the Duke's most valuable adviser. Duke Ting was not famous for his energetic attention to his duties. One day he asked Confucius idly, "Isn't there one sentence that could make a country rich?"

"You can't expect that from one sentence," replied the Master. "Still, there is a saying, 'To be a prince is difficult, to be a minister far from easy.' A prince who really applied himself to being a prince in every sense of the word—well, his country would grow rich."

Duke Ting hastily thought up another question: "Well, isn't there one sentence that could ruin a country?"

"Not one sentence," said Confucius. "But there is a saying, 'The finest thing about being a prince is that, when he speaks, nobody disagrees.' Now if this prince made certain that he spoke only words of wisdom, and nobody disagreed, that would be a fine thing. But if he spoke nonsense and nobody disagreed—that would ruin a country, soon enough!"

Let us assume that Confucius might have rebuilt the realm of Chou if only he had been allowed to continue governing, regulating, and igniting wisdom in Duke Ting. However, across the border to the north, he was arousing enmity. His old admirer, Duke Ching of Ch'i, was beginning to look with alarm at the growing prosperity of Lu. One of the main reasons why Ch'i was always hospitable to little Lu's political refugees was that Ch'i profited by trouble in Lu. There were fortresses and territories on the border between the two states that, when Lu was weak, could be occupied by Ch'i. And when Lu grew strong, they would inevitably be snatched back by Lu.

Now in the spring of 500 B.C., the Duke of Ch'i, wishing to parley with the Duke of Lu and perhaps to assassinate his chief minister, Master K'ung, should an opportunity occur, invited Ting to a meeting at a spot near the border. Of course, the event was represented as a simple reunion to cement the friendly relations that existed between their two countries. Duke Ting was happy as a child going to a picnic. He ordered his informal chariot, the one he loved to drive himself, to be made ready.

Confucius took a more suspicious view of the affair. He uttered, perhaps for the first time in history, the renowned dictum of the practical politician: "If you want peace, prepare for war." This durable maxim sped around the earth and eventually came to the ears of the poet Horace in Rome, later still to George Washington, and still later to Anthony Eden when he was Prime Minister of England. Indeed, in our own atomic age, the saying is the keynote of practical politics.

Confucius said to his Duke, "When princes cross the borders of their native lands, they should take with them their entire official retinue." Gently prodding, he got Ting to set forth in great state with chariots, dignitaries, guardsmen, and the Marshals of the Right and the Left. When they arrived at the picnic site, they were heartily glad of their panoply, for Duke Ching had brought all of his ministers and marshals with him too. Furthermore, he had planned a most elaborate sort of party. A special terrace had been built, with a high platform, which was reached by ascending a triple stairway. Atop the platform, quite removed from the multitude, places were set for the two rulers, where clever Ching and silly Ting could talk over affairs of state without the unwelcome advice of ministers.

The princes met and bowed, offering each other precedence up the central staircase. Ascending side by side to the top, they found refreshments waiting, and they drank to each other, bowing, exchanging compliments and expressions of goodwill. Then they sat down and began their conversation.

Presently an official of Ch'i advanced up the stairs and said, "I beg that the music be performed."

"Let it be performed," said Ching of Ch'i with a gracious smile.

Dancers appeared in the grove below. They were barbarian vassals, dressed in wild costumes with feathers and animal tails, and they screamed and stamped and beat their drums, waving their hands and sticks. Close scrutiny revealed that they were also carrying spears and lances, swords and shields, and were advancing ominously close to the spot where the officials from Lu were enjoying the gracious hospitality of their counterparts from Ch'i.

Confucius missed nothing. He detached himself from the group, and hastening forward, mounted the staircase at a swift pace, stopping at the next-to-the-last step. Even in an emergency—and he had perceived that it was an emergency—he would not set foot upon the sacred princely platform. He stood still, raised his sleeve, and said, "Our two princes are here for a friendly meeting.

What are these noisy barbarians doing here? I beg that they be removed."

All eyes were turning on Duke Ching, who blushed hotly to have been caught in such a crude trick. Sheepishly, he commanded that the dancers leave the grove.

Again the Dukes engaged in conversation, and again an official of Ch'i came forward, saying, "I request that the music of the inner palace be performed."

Duke Ching again consented, but instead of soft-handed musicians, there burst upon the sight a jolly company of jugglers and dwarfs with their odd dances and comic antics and also clubs, sticks, robes, and throwing knives. In half a minute, everything was noise and confusion, enough to camouflage the most horrendous deeds. Confucius, moving alertly, mounted the steps with as much dignity as speed allowed, and standing on the next-to-the-last step, he said, "It is a crime meriting death to disturb princes in their talk. I beg that the dancers be removed."

Duke Ching was now ready to fall through the floor with embarrassment. Such was Confucius' massive dignity that he felt he had been reprimanded for bad taste. He descended from the platform and proceeded to blame everything on his officials saying, "You with your barbarians and jugglers! In Lu they know what befits the dignity of a prince. Now that you have put me in the wrong, what are we going to do next?"

An official stepped forward and said, "If a person of noble character has committed a fault, he excuses himself with action. A person of low character excuses himself with words alone."

Ching was pleased with this advice which showed that great-hearted wisdom was not absent from the state of Ch'i. He returned to the platform and told Ting he would give back much of the territory he had recently stolen from Lu.

In this way Confucius won a diplomatic victory for his prince, besides showing future generations that, while princes conversed, they must never be interrupted, and if they were, it must be from the next-to-the-last step.

8. *"When I Was Fifty..."*

"When I was fifty,
I recognized that Heaven had a will of its own."

Some vivid traditions survive to show us a living picture of Confucius in these brief days of his fame when he is said to have filled a high post as a government official.

"His manner, usually, was simple and amiable, and he was so shy with words that one would have thought him hardly able to speak. But at court and temple he spoke up clearly and in detail—though he never spoke too much. When conversing with officials lower in rank, he was friendly and straightforward. When speaking of those of higher grade, he was amiable and informative. When the ruler was present, his manner was grave but self-possessed.

"As he spoke, he bent toward the others, moving his folded hands to the left or right, but always keeping the skirts of his robe before and behind evenly adjusted.

"When the Duke called him forward, he moved quickly, holding his arms like the wings of a bird. When the Duke asked him to receive a visitor, his face seemed to change expression and his legs to move forward with difficulty. When he entered the palace gates, he bowed his head respectfully. He never allowed himself to stand in the middle of the threshold or even to tread directly on it."

If some of these vignettes of the Master show him, in our eyes, over-respectful toward the throne, we must remember two things: first, he was a man of enormous personal magnetism, and he knew it; second, he was determined to call attention to the respect owed to the ducal crown. It was a lesson not only to the frivolous and privileged noblemen, but to the rising class of military knights, the "new blood" at court, that when he passed the vacant throne of the Duke, "his countenance changed, his legs buckled, and his words came as if he hardly had breath to utter them.

"He ascended the steps of the throne holding his robe with both hands, his body bent. He held his breath as if he dared not breathe, but the moment he left the audience, at the very first step he began to relax and to look satisfied. At the bottom of the steps he returned to his place quickly, his arms held like wings. . . ."

People never forgot this show put on by Confucius. They also remembered the private Confucius, a man of many eccentricities and foibles, but none contrary to the instincts of a gentleman who practiced modest luxury, with a complete absence of ostentation.

He never dressed in flashy colors, purple or red or reddish, even at home. He preferred black. In summer he wore a black robe over an inner garment, and in winter over lamb's fur he wore black. If he wore fawn-colored fur, he preferred a white robe. His most flamboyant costume was a yellow robe worn over the fur of fox.

All of these garments were varied according to the

occasion. When he fasted for ritual purposes, his clothes had to be clean white linen. His ordinary housecoat had the right sleeve cut short for practicality.

He was fastidious about his food. The rice had to be very well cleaned and his meat cut small. He never ate rice that had been spoiled by heat or damp or bought at the public market, nor any meat that was not quite fresh, nor anything discolored or badly cooked or out of season.

He wouldn't sit down to eat at all unless his mat was straight.

The sauce on his meat had to be the right sauce for the dish, and he never took more than was proportionate to a moderate helping of rice. He had no rules about wine; still, no one ever saw him drunk.

Whatever he ate of, he offered a little first in grave sacrifice to his ancestors.

Numerous recollections show his regard for the concerns of others. When, traveling through the villages, he found the countryfolk performing a ceremony at a temple, on behalf of crops or an illness or a local crisis, he would take the trouble to put on his formal robes and stand on the side steps of the temple.

When a friend died and there were no relations to perform the rites, he would say, "I will bury him."

Once he returned home to find that his stable had burned down. Confucius said, "Was anyone hurt?" His first thought was not for his property.

In great ways and in small ways, this orphan boy had shaped himself into the universal model of a gentleman:

the great-hearted humanist who is the crowning glory of a liberal education. Such a man places the correct value on himself and on everything about him. Easy of manner, he wears a pleasant expression that hides private feelings —though on occasion he might rise up in righteous wrath. He talks freely and agreeably, but he does not babble. He keeps private matters and grave matters to himself. He greets distinguished acquaintances and humble ones with the same unselfconscious respect. He doesn't point or shout or turn his head around to stare. He does not talk behind people's backs. He never says a word to humiliate others, and he cannot be humiliated. He has no prejudices, no obstinacy, and no egoism.

All of these qualities were noted in Confucius. Of course, even the greatest gentleman has little weaknesses. We are told that the Master was frightened of thunder and grew pale at sudden gusts of wind.

Long before the days of Confucius, the black-haired people had noted the evils of uncontrolled armaments, and laws had been made to limit the stockpiling of deadly weapons. Strictly speaking, no state in the Chou realm could own more than a thousand war chariots, and no individual family could own more than a hundred. The walls of fortified cities could have only so many openings for shooting and pouring boiling oil. However, by the end of the Spring and Autumn Period, people were forgetting all about these rules.

Confucius made a comment on this matter of deadly weapons that should be treated as eternal wisdom. "Maintaining a country of a thousand chariots," he warned, "calls for complete honesty, earnestness, thrift, fair employment regulations, and love for one's fellowman."

In his heyday as a high official of Lu, he tackled the matter practically. "We can't have officials," he told Duke Ting, "who keep concealed stores of weapons. And the noble families must not maintain fortified cities with walls more than three thousand feet long."

This was a frontal attack against the military might of the Three Families, who in recent generations had been building strongholds at vulnerable points throughout the land which served them as bases of power where their troops were garrisoned and their armories piled up. Confucius now foisted his own disciple, Tze Lu, on the Chi family as a steward, and Tze Lu was under secret orders to dismantle their fortified cities.

Tze Lu used a wily argument. In such rebellious times, he said, with so many discontented vassals constantly seizing the fortresses and using them as bases for revolt, the fortifications were more trouble than they were worth. How mild the feudal lords had become under the rule of Confucius is seen in the fact that the Chi accepted this reasoning and began to tear down their walls. The Shu did not wait to be prodded but dismantled their fortifications.

The Meng remained. They argued back. They said that Lu needed their chief fortified city for defense purposes since it was close to the border.

Then suddenly trouble broke loose. Some malcontent vassal knights who had really hoped to use these cities for trouble saw what was being done to them, and they rose up against Duke Ting, the Chi, the Shu, the Meng, Confucius, and every other form of authority in the land.

Confucius had the army well in hand; this rebellion was soon put down, and the dismantling of fortifications proceeded. But rebellion boiled again and again. Confucius indeed had overreached himself, as happens often with energetic politicians, failing to gauge the hotheaded temper of the rebels. In the time gained, the forces of oppression collected themselves. The Three Families had a chance to reflect and perceive that Confucius had hoodwinked them. Previously they had trusted him to preserve their established privileges, but now they saw him for what he was: a reformer, a radical, who did not care about the Three Families. From this time on, they conspired against him.

But before these enmities came out into the open, Confucius enjoyed triumph in Lu. He pacified the rebellious knights; he made his precious Duke a present of authority such as the throne had not enjoyed for generations, and the grateful Ting rewarded him with the supreme office, that of acting chancellor of Lu. He was in his early fifties, and before him there stretched years of happy activity, as little by little he would cause the honor of the Chou to shine again—and, who knows, perhaps rebuild their kingdom out of little Lu.

Ardently in love with a noble heritage, he set to work to rule Lu. And so well did he rule that we are told the sellers of lambs and of suckling pigs no longer falsified their prices. Lost objects lying in the streets were not picked up, but were left there for their owners to come back and find them. Foreigners visiting the state did not need to turn to officials to find out where they might spend the night without being robbed or murdered. Every house in the land stood open to them, as safe as if they were returning to their own homes.

As for the rules of propriety, the men of Lu walked on one side of the street, and the women walked on the other.

Happiness shone out of Confucius. His disciples were amused. "We have heard it said by a certain sage," they teased him, "that a Superior Man in hard times does not fear and in good times does not jump for joy."

"Ah, yes, you have heard it," replied Confucius. "But naturally, a Superior Man doesn't mind unbending among his friends."

What a good thing it was for Confucius that by his own words he had learned that Heaven had a will of its own. He soon found that it did not necessarily coincide with the will of acting chancellors. For throughout these happy times, in the state of Ch'i to the north, Duke Ching was becoming seriously alarmed. Everywhere people were talking about what a fortunate state Lu was to live in. Ching said to his ministers, "Soon Confucius will be the most powerful man in the east, and if he chooses to annex land, whose land is next door? Ours is. Perhaps we ought to offer him more land before he seizes it."

His prime minister was more cautious. "First, let's see

if we can't put a stop to him. If we can't, then there will be time to offer him more land."

Like any good prime minister, he knew that to destroy an enemy he must first find out his weak points. What was the weakest point of Confucius? He did not appear to have one. He was good at everything, strong in everything, fortunate in everything.

But after some thought, the answer came quite easily: the weak point of Confucius was Duke Ting.

Intrigues were set in motion. The traditions suggest that the Three Families of Lu did not hesitate to work hand in glove with the ministers of Ch'i to manufacture the doom of Confucius.

First, the towns, villages, and noble harems of Ch'i were combed, and from them all the loveliest girls in the land were selected and brought by the hundreds to the capital to be scrutinized by the ministers. And then this crowd of girls was combed through again and a new selection made until only eighty were left, all of them like glorious angels, and they were scrubbed until they glowed, rubbed until they shone, and painted until they dazzled the sight.

Every morning the girls were wakened early and made to practice musical instruments. Then, after they were fed, they were given dancing lessons, and later in the day, they were taught to sing. And at last, they were put to bed. After some time they turned into the most interesting bevy of damsels ever to trip down the garden paths of China, and when they seemed quite perfect in every way, they were dressed in costly garments, given thirty sets of magnificent steeds, and all in glittering caparison sent as a gift to Duke Ting of Lu.

During his time of power, while Confucius had been causing the men of Lu to walk on a different side of the street from the women, he had by no means neglected the morals of Duke Ting. "He who loves hunting and women abandons his state to ruin" was the sort of thing he said to him. And also, "A happy union with wife and children is like the music of lutes and harps."

On the whole he had managed well, keeping the Duke too busy to have much thought beyond his legitimate wives. But now, on that shocking day when the maidens and their steeds appeared at the South High Gate of Ch'u-fu, the Duke was consumed by curiosity. Of course, he did not confess his thoughts to Confucius; he told them to Baron Huan of Chi. The Baron offered to go down to the South High Gate and observe the girls, and he did so. After some time he came away, but three times he returned, as if drawn by a powerful magnet. Then he reported his impressions of the display of feminine and equine beauty to Duke Ting.

The Duke called for his chariot to go for a drive, and he directed the charioteer to veer toward the South High Gate. He did not return to his duties that day.

Tze Lu, who was a realist, gloomily summarized the situation. "Well," he said to Confucius, "we might as well take ourselves off."

Confucius had faith in his Duke. He refused to believe that Ting would not show up for the rites which were to take place on the following day. "There is to be a sacrificial feast in the square," he said. "If the Duke sends the proper gifts of sacrificial meat to the dignitaries, I'll overlook what has happened."

The sacrifice took place. The Duke neither came nor sent the dignitaries their dinner.

Looking back on these far-off events, nothing could seem less important to our eyes than that these seemingly empty actions should take place. Yet they were enormously important, because they changed the whole history of the black-haired people. To Confucius, the importance of the ritual, the Mass for the state, was such that the Duke's failure to attend was an unanswerable insult. There was only one dignified course of action: to resign his office, go into exile, separate himself from his beloved Lu.

He left that day. He traveled northwestward toward the state of Wei, and with him went some faithful disciples and friends. They did not stop until they reached the frontier; then, in a village, they took lodging for the night.

The Master bedded down in a room by himself to nurse his grief and perhaps to hope for a message from Ting calling him back. But no message came.

Then a knock came at the door. It was an old man, a frontier guard, who said, "I always make a point of calling on great personages who pass this way." Confucius put aside his feelings to receive the man and chat with him awhile. On his way out, passing through the room where the friends and disciples sat, despondently, the visitor paused and said, "Why are you moaning that your Master has lost his office? The whole world lives in ignorance. Now your Master will call out instruction." He rather spoiled these well-meant remarks by adding, "Now he is only a wooden-tongued bell!"

With such cold comfort did Confucius leave Lu. His friend of many years, the Music Master of Lu, had come with him thus far, though he was old and blind and the way was hard for him. He said lamely, "It wasn't your fault, Master K'ung."

"Shall I sing you a song?" said Confucius, and he raised his voice:

> "It is women's songs
> That foiled me,
> And women's smiles
> Despoiled me.
> Oh woe, oh wandering,
> Unto life's end."

9. "Wherever Could My Master Go ..."

"Wherever could my Master go and not become educated?"

A glance at the map will show that the state of Wei toward which the deposed sage was directing his steps was, like Lu, one of the smallest of the central states. Being a little closer to the Chou capital at Loyang, in the heart of the realm, it might perhaps be judged a more sophisticated place. Certainly the men of Wei did not walk on the opposite side of the street from the ladies. They preferred to imitate their ruler, Duke Ling, who had never in his life avoided women and now, in his old age, was putty in the hands of his favorite wife, Nan Tze.

Confucius arrived in Wei about 497 B.C., when he was fifty-four years old. With him were several disciples. The ones chiefly mentioned as sharing his exile were the straitlaced Tze Lu, his greatest friend; the suave diplomat Tze Kung; and Yen Hui, the most brilliant of the disciples, a modest, gentle person, so sparing of words that even the Master did not quite understand him, though he loved Yen Hui more than he loved his own son.

Tze Lu had a brother-in-law in Wei, and the refugees

lodged in his house, while Confucius hopefully waited for Duke Ling of Wei to summon him and offer him a post in government.

A summons was not long in coming. The Duke was overjoyed to have such an amusing man at his court. "What was your salary in Lu?" he wanted to know.

"I received sixty thousand bushels of grain," replied Confucius.

"I'll give you the same," said Duke Ling. However, he did not say a word about offering Confucius a post with duties or responsibilities.

The presence of the Master created a stir at the court of Wei, where his undistinguished birth excited curiosity. One noble, perhaps with a lurking sneer, asked Tze Kung, "Where did your Master gain his education?"

The urbane and charming Tze Kung had a well-polished reply: "The spirit of the ancient Chou did not die with them. It was preserved in our race. Their greatness is present in our great-minded men; their faults are present in our small-minded men. Wherever could my Master go and not be educated?"

The buzz of gossip extended to the inner courts of the palace where Nan Tze, the notorious favorite, held sway. The bounds of this woman's infamy, which did not stop at adultery, murder, and infanticide, are far beyond the reach of this book to describe. She and her frightful young men were the real rulers of Wei. The aged Duke Ling doted on the woman. It would have been wise of Confucius to have called upon Nan Tze, improper as such

a meeting between honorable sage and disgraceful fe-
male would have been. Of course he did not dream of it.
And so, Nan Tze was obliged to summon him herself.
She did so with studied elegance: "The lords of the lands
that deign to conclude brotherhood with our Duke
usually call upon my insignificant self. My insignificance
desires to see Master K'ung also."

The old chroniclers do not describe for us the mood
with which Confucius received this message. We can only
guess his outrage and his sleepless night. He certainly did
not dare to ask the advice of Tze Lu. Indeed, he spared
all of his company embarrassment by not saying one
word about the summons, but at the appointed time he
went forth alone to the inner court of the palace, salvaging
whatever he could of dignity by an extreme display of
formal manners. Entering the door of the Lady Nan
Tze's reception hall, he bowed ceremoniously toward the
north, and then advanced and stood silently, staring at
the tiles of the floor, not raising his eyes.

Nan Tze sat behind a curtain. She had wished to see
Confucius, and now she was seeing him, scrutinizing him
carefully through a hole in the embroidery. In returning
his salutation, she waved her hands twice, making certain
that he heard her jade bangles tinkling against each other.
No words were exchanged. That would have been too
improper, even for Nan Tze.

After allowing himself to be examined for a polite
interval, Confucius bowed and left. Back in his lodgings,
he found his following in an uproar, appalled by what he

had done. "I didn't want to go! I had to!" he defended himself. "And after all, she behaved herself very decorously."

Tze Lu, however, was in a state of towering indignation, especially as he guessed that by going alone Confucius had deliberately drawn the gossip on his own head, sparing theirs. His reproaches were such that Confucius was reduced to placating him, over and over, "Whatever I did, Heaven forced me! Heaven forced me!"

Perhaps it was from the courts of Nan Tze that the whisper went forth that was to spoil the life of Confucius in Wei. She could not have welcomed his efforts to imbue the mind of her Duke with novel ideas of government. Before long, a suspicion spread abroad that Confucius was not altogether a man to be trusted. To be sure, he seemed to be an innocent sage in exile, but these were troubled times, and he might well have been a secret agent in the pay of the state of Lu.

Duke Ling must have taken this notion seriously, because he caused an agent of his own to shadow the Master and his disciples wherever they went, observing what they did and to whom they spoke.

Confucius found this shadow so humiliating that he gave up the idea of establishing a home in Wei and set forth again across the land. From this time there began for him long years of wandering across the valley of the Huang Ho. Occasionally he would return to Wei to rest with Tze Lu's hospitable relatives. He was always welcomed happily by Duke Ling, who had taken a great fancy to him. And so the sage would stay until sheer boredom or exasperation with the Duke's disastrous love life sent him fleeing again across the river valley.

The memory of one painful episode remains to show us what Confucius must have suffered in Wei. One day the Duke invited him to go driving in town, and, of course, he accepted with pleasure, happy for the opportunity to pour improving notions about the township's problems into the ear of Duke Ling. But upon arriving at the palace gates where the royal carriage awaited, he found two carriages standing there. The first, garlanded and beribboned for the occasion, was just being mounted by the Duke, who, with an expression of senile delight on his face, was handing in beside him the simpering, fluttering Nan Tze. Confucius was obliged to mount the second, lesser carriage. And thus they drove around the open market for all to witness his second-rate standing.

Master K'ung, being a Superior Man, let none read by his expression resentment of this slight. But he discharged his feelings with one immortal comment: "I have never met a man who put excellence above prettiness."

Then, he collected his household and left gay Wei.

10. "Those Who Leave Their Native Lands..."

"Those who leave their native lands are like a river—never stopping, always rushing, day and night."

Confucius spent his years of wandering in search of a prince who would employ him. On the basis of the accounts at our disposal, his travels are impossible to follow either geographically or chronologically. The numerous anecdotes and episodes that remain to us seem disconnected, or they are linked without reason, and they often overlap and double back in time. They are threaded through with his sorrow and homesickness for his native land.

Wherever he went, princes, ministers, and court officials would pounce on him and question him about the proper conduct of government; but they did not take his ideas to heart, and none offered him a post in government. In later centuries, Confucian scholars found it incredible that rulers who could have availed themselves of the Master's wisdom were deaf to it. Still, looking back judiciously, it is easy to see that with everything to gain by war and taxes, these feudal princes did not want **to**

78

saddle themselves with a sage who would only tell them with tiresome repetitiousness: "The art of government consists in making people happy."

He traveled with a retinue of pupils, and their ranks were swelled along the way by other young men, drawn by his growing fame as a teacher. Although this movable household did not live lavishly, they did not suffer want, and nothing in the tradition shows that the Master ordinarily went hungry. They must have suffered the usual hardships of travelers, but Confucius held discomfort to be beneath the notice of superior men.

There were adventures along the way, and as year by year the countryside became more unsettled by repeated wars and danger of war, there were perils also. Once, the citizens of a town, observing Confucius' huge size and fearsome visage, jumped to the conclusion that he could only be that other famous giant of the times, Yang Hu. The former dictator, after his escape from Lu, had made his living by banditry, and was busy sacking and plundering fortresses up and down the land. A crowd quickly gathered, seized Confucius, and dragged him off to prison. In the ensuing days, his company of disciples was rounded up one by one and brought to share his confinement. After five days, the young man Yen Hui was brought in, to the Master's huge relief. "I thought you were dead!" he cried.

Yen Hui then delivered the fond reply that won him immortal fame among Chinese schoolboys and their masters: "So long as my Master lives, how could I dare to die?"

The townspeople refused to give up their suspicions, and the disciples were terrified that some hot-tempered oaf would put an end to the Master's life. Confucius was quite calm. At ordinary times, he tended to speak of himself ironically, as if he were a pupil at the bottom of his own class. But in this perilous moment, he showed a mystic sense of his importance. "Since King Wen is dead," he said, "this civilization is entrusted to my keeping. Had Heaven wished to destroy it, it would have done so long ago, and we should never have had the chance to educate ourselves. But obviously Heaven wishes to preserve it. What, therefore, can these people do to me?"

Feeling the hand of destiny protecting them, they endured their ordeal. Meanwhile, back in Wei, practical measures were being undertaken to rescue them. A former pupil of Confucius swiftly joined the diplomatic corps of Wei, and from this position of influence was able to negotiate for their release.

On another occasion it was one of the rich pupils who placed the company in jeopardy. The event occurred in Sung, a state that above all others ought to have honored Confucius, since it was the homeland of his ancestors. However, at that time it was ruled by a military dictator, and this man's younger brother had recently left his useful army life to join Confucius' band as a disciple, where goodness knows what pacifistic notions were being poured into his innocent ears.

Happily, the dictator could think of no better way of putting an end to the Master than by sending a band of soldiers to sneak up behind him and hack down a tree under which he was lecturing to his pupils. All the company were alert enough to see the danger and agile enough to jump out of the way. They fled into the forest, and Confucius again made a statement of faith: "Heaven has generated the spirit in me. This man cannot harm me."

They decided to separate, each man to make his own way to safety across the border of Sung. Arriving alone in the neighboring state, Confucius stood hesitantly at the gates of a town, wondering how he would find his company again. A townsman, who had previously encountered Tze Kung inquiring everywhere for news of the Master, reported back: "At the East Gate there stands a man with a brow like a hero and a neck the same. But from the waist down, he sags. He stands there as glum as a dog at a funeral."

When Tze Kung, having joined the Master, told him of this description, Confucius laughed aloud and said, "I don't know about my heroic torso, but the dog at a funeral—that fits, that fits!"

The years went by. In peace and war, in flood and famine, they crisscrossed the valley of the Huang Ho, and we read of their traveling through Ch'u, Cheng, Wu, P'u, Tsin, Ts'ai, Ts'ao, and many other little states and fortified towns that clung to the riverside. Wherever the Master went, he visited libraries, burying himself in the great moldering, wormy volumes that had lain for centuries on crumbling shelves. In time, no one questioned that he was easily the most learned man in the world. The princes often consulted him on points of ceremonial, history, tradition, and portents. His replies seem to us fabulous, like scrolls unrolling from the beginning of time, crowded with the lore of the primeval world.

Once the Duke of Ch'en sent to him urgently to pronounce the meaning of a strange event. A sparrow hawk had lighted on the roof of the palace and died. It was found to have been pierced with a strange arrow made of *hou*-wood, one foot, eight inches long, and with a stone head.

Confucius said without hesitation: "The arrow was made by the Su Shen barbarians."

Then he went on to explain how he knew: "After King Wu overcame the Yin Dynasty, he extended his power over far-flung tribes and caused them all to appear before him, bringing as tributes the goods of their native lands. The Su Shen brought arrows of *hou*-wood with stone heads. They were one foot, eight inches long.

"Then the great king, in order to show his wide influence, caused all these gifts, brought from the most distant lands, to be redistributed among the principal families of all the tribes to remind them of the realm's immensity. These arrows of the Su Shen were brought here when the King's own daughter married a duke of this state. That is why they are still to be found occasionally in these parts."

Such statements, describing events that had taken place six centuries back, when checked in the local archives were found to be correct.

Once Tze Kung was asked how Confucius managed to learn so much about the administration of states through which he passed: "Does he demand information, or is it given him?"

Tze Kung replied, "He gets it through a gentle willingness to listen."

This habit of not talking much himself, but drawing forth from others all they knew, reinforced the suspicion some people had that Confucius was a spy in the pay of some potentate, and as unrest spread across the land, this was a dangerous reputation. Once, returning to Wei through P'u, a fortified town whose populace was in full rebellion—even the women were joining in the fighting —the people of P'u decided they would feel much safer if Confucius were in prison, out of mischief. They were about to arrest him when, just in time, there arrived upon the scene a rich disciple accompanied by five chariots with armed men in them. "I'll fight to the death rather than see my Master put in jail," announced this young man, and he fought so fiercely that the citizens of P'u agreed to release Confucius, but they made him promise, on oath, that he would not return to Wei and disclose their military operations to Duke Ling. Confucius swore the oath.

In all feudal societies, oaths are highly valued, a man's word of honor being often more stable than the law. Tze Kung was therefore horrified when, once outside the border of P'u, Confucius doubled back in the direction of Wei.

"An extorted oath," he explained, "may be broken. The gods do not hear it." Once more, he was making his own rules, impatient of the conventions of feudal society.

Duke Ling of Wei was so pleased at the Master's safe escape from P'u that he traveled out of his city a good way to meet him, entertaining himself on the road by plotting a war of conquest against P'u. "Can P'u be attacked?" he asked excitedly.

"Oh, yes," said Confucius, and he deliberately violated his oath by telling the Duke all the military dispositions he had observed, probably knowing that the Duke would not attack in any case. Duke Ling was very old, and such war games were only dreams; he left all details of government to Nan Tze. He liked Confucius to buzz in his ear about politics, but he had no real interest in anything he said. One day, as the two friends sat in the royal garden while the Master tried to explain some subtle point of policy to him, the Duke's glance was caught by a wild goose flying, and followed the bird across the sky. Confucius caught him with his head in the clouds, and it quite depressed him that even old Ling had no use for his wisdom.

Shortly after that, Duke Ling died. The ensuing squabbles in Wei, as Nan Tze and her disorderly clique jostled and plotted for power, set Confucius gypsying forth again across the troubled realm where burned castles and looted temples, barren fields and mourning families were commonplace. Pitying the prostrate countryside, Confucius said, "If only someone would make use of me, something would be seen in a year and a day, and in three years I could have everything restored."

And he flung out his disappointment: "Am I only a gourd to be hung up to dry out without being eaten?"

He longed to be recalled to Lu. In 494, his old faulty prince, Duke Ting, had died, and was succeeded by Duke Ai. Knowing full well how badly his country needed prosperous guidance, Confucius had waited in vain to be recalled by the new Duke. But he was not recalled. Baron Huan, the head of the Chi family, who had worked the mischief against him, was chancellor, and he ruled Lu.

Then in 490, Baron Huan fell ill, and on his deathbed he meditated, with repentance, upon the past years. "There was a time," he said, "when this state was at the peak of prosperity. Those were the days of Master K'ung. Now it is so no longer. I was at fault when I conspired against the Master."

He called his heir, Baron K'ung, and said, "When I die, you will succeed to my office. Promise me that you will summon Master K'ung."

Baron K'ang gave this promise, and when his father died, he would indeed have recalled Confucius to Lu. But one of his counselors spoke out against it: "Once Duke Ting, our departed lord, appointed him. But his ideas were too extreme and his plans so radical that none of them could be carried through. Every prince in the realm was laughing at us."

He persuaded K'ang that to honor the spirit of the promise he had made to his father, he should recall, instead of Confucius, one of his prominent disciples, Jan Ch'iu. Now Jan Ch'iu was a brilliant young man about thirty years old, but he was not a favorite of the Master, who considered him to be opportunistic and self-seeking. When, therefore, the messengers came from

Lu, the Master was apprehensive. "When Jan Ch'iu is summoned home," he said, "it must be for an important reason."

Later, when he found that Jan Ch'iu had been recalled to fill a high position, he did not contain his mixed feelings of pride and disappointment: "My pupils are brilliant, skilled in all the arts—they will do great things with their lives. But when they go away from me, will they go on learning and training themselves?"

And he added, "Oh, I want to go home! I want to go home!"

Before Jan Ch'iu went back to Lu, Tze Kung paid him a visit and said to him privately, "Just make sure that as soon as you can, you will find a way to recall the Master."

But year followed year, and no word came from Jan Ch'iu.

THE TEACHING

Heaven and Human Nature

The more I look at his teaching, the higher it rises before me; the more I try to penetrate it, the more impenetrable does it become. I see it spread out before me, then suddenly it is behind me; but when the Master explains he puts everything in place.

He has expanded me with knowledge, he has shaped me with discipline. Even if I wished to give up, I could not; for whenever I become tired of learning, the Master's excellence, his grandeur fills my mind, and I know that I must follow him—though I can never follow him all the way.

—YEN HUI

In centuries to come, the biographers of Confucius would write with pathos about the sad, homeless wanderer, toiling across the face of a countryside seething with robbers and rebels. Yet, perhaps the Master does not need our sympathy more than anyone else condemned to live away from a beloved home. He was, after all, not an ordinary political refugee but a distinguished exile, who was generally received at castles and courts with respect,

89

curiosity, and even, after they got used to him, with a friendly welcome. As Tze Kung said, one might just as well try to deny the light of the sun and the moon as deny the charm of Confucius.

When Confucius left Lu, he was middle-aged; before he was able to go back, he was old. It was during those years of full maturity, bitter years for him of repeated frustrations and seeming failure, that his philosophy took shape and became known up and down the valley of the Huang Ho, among men who admired his wit, even if they did not listen to his wisdom.

Confucius was by nature sparing with words. It is possible that the inconvenience of his nomadic existence prompted him to frame his thoughts even more sharply, in phrases that could be carried about in heads instead of in wooden books. No doubt his disciples—who by this time hailed from all parts of the Chou realm—treasured and memorized what he said. After his death they made a collection called the *Lun Yü,* or, as it is usually translated into English, the *Analects.* Both titles mean simply "collected sayings." The *Lun Yü* became one of the most important of the Confucian classics. The sayings, with their sound observations and common sense, were like small strong seeds that could grow in everyman's garden. Together with other writings said to have been penned by the Master in his old age, or by later scholars from memory, they form the framework of the ethical, social, and political system known in history as "Confucianism" which endured for more than two thousand years. In time, the teachings came to be called the "Constitution of China."

Yet, when the Master lived and taught, he did not mean his notions to be used for ruling so much as for civilizing. His practical aim was to show everyone of high and low degree how they ought to think and behave for their own good and the good of the community. That a political scheme developed was a by-product of his basic premise: that the harmonies of nature can be made to prevail in all of man's works.

Since the Chinese revolution of 1912, Confucius as a political tool has withdrawn into the shadows of history. But the strong humane and ethical character of the teachings, stamped upon them by the personality of the Master, has not withered; it is ingrained in cultural traditions. Among the Chinese people at large and the cognate races of Korea, Japan, and Indochina what is meant by such concepts as "gentleman" or "virtue" or "superiority" is very much as Confucius would have hoped.

The teachings of Confucius begin with a belief in Heaven; they end with a splendid portrait of a man.

The Great Learning

Confucius was a humanist, a lover of man. In his philosophy, humankind has the star role, and man's earthly life is the stage. The main theme is the development of the individual, and next to that the welfare of people: their prosperity, safety, and education. Benevolence is the word that characterizes his point of view, just as compassion marks the thought of Gautama Buddha, and love that of Jesus Christ.

Unlike the great spiritual teachers, Confucius was not concerned with such matters as the meaning of life and death or the destiny of the soul. The only reward he offers to one who follows his teaching is the feeling of peace that comes from having made use of his life well.

Yet Heaven is not absent from the thought of Confucius. The Master said, "Heaven and Earth are separate, but the work they do is the same." He sees man as the instrument, as well as the fine child of a union between intelligence and matter. He is the equal of his parents, a member of a trinity. Just as intelligence breathes life into matter, so man, by exercising his own intelligence, shapes the world about him.

In the book called *Ta Hsüeh,* or the *Great Learning,* the Master described in a parable how necessity forces man to think, and how the inner world of thought becomes translated into the outer world of things.

"The ancient kings who originally put our world in order began by regulating their kingdoms. Wishing to regulate their kingdoms they began by regulating their own families. Wishing to regulate their families, they ennobled their lives. In ennobling their lives, they purified their thoughts. In purifying their thoughts, they cultivated their minds. In cultivating their minds, they extended to the utmost their knowledge. In extending their knowledge, they grasped the nature of things.

"And when they had grasped the nature of things, their

knowledge was complete. Knowledge being complete, their minds were cultivated. Minds being cultivated, their thoughts became pure, and with the purification of thought, their lives were ennobled. Their lives being ennobled, their families were regulated, and their families being regulated, order reigned in their states. Consequently, there was peace on earth."

In these two paragraphs, as sparse and simple as a child's rhyme, the Master traced a path between the material and the divine; he knitted intellectual values with moral ones, and in the center he firmly planted creative man, who, by achieving perfection in himself, automatically perfects his society.

With this thought he had said enough to carry his notions beyond the tiled courts of ancient princes into the mainstream of speculative thought.

Of the matters that exist between man and Heaven, Confucius also said: "If Heaven and Earth had no intercommunication, things would not grow and flourish the way they do."

And he said:

"Of all that Heaven has produced and Earth nourishes, the greatest is man."

The Li

"How majestically did King Shun rule his empire," Confucius said to his pupils. "As if he barely noticed it was there."

He did not mean to praise the hero-king's patrician

indifference, but his absolutely correct, harmonious conduct. This, radiating from the ruler, imbued every as-
pect of government, so that affairs of state ran on well-
oiled wheels. The right conduct of the king set in motion
a pattern of exact action.

It is only when earthly patterns match Heaven's that
the spiritual beings which make up Heaven can be drawn
into the drama of man and made to operate helpfully on
earth. Ancestral ghosts, elementals of air, water, fire, and
earth, devas of the mountains and demons of the caves, all
of these, attracted by earthly virtue, are compelled to
perform the beneficent duties Heaven's sublime pattern imposes on them. They keep great rivers flowing
in their proper courses and winds blowing from the
right direction, bringing rain where and when it is
wanted; and they send running across the broad acres of
black soil little fairy animals that cause the crops to teem,
so that prosperous farmers, feeling well-rewarded for their
labors, gladly pay their tithes to their overlords; and
the overlords, in their turn infected with virtue, naturally use their money to cultivate the arts, to enrich,
rejoice, and educate their underlings, and to serve the
king.

There was a beautiful circularity to the ideal world of
Confucius, one excellent situation leading to another, so
that when he spoke of King Shun, he was able to express,
with the brevity he loved, the germ of perfect government: "What, after all, did the king do? He watched
his conduct carefully and turned his face southward

solemnly. Nothing more." The king respected himself and feared Heaven; this was majesty.

Confucius had no doubt that transcendental harmony existed and powerfully affected the world's affairs. He was an artist, and he could see it—in the orderly, workings of nature, in the rhythms of music and poetry, in the growth of plants and the ways of animals, in the motion of stars, in the works of man.

Harmony, unity, order—these were the blazing truths underlying the nature of things. This was the ancient golden secret. Trouble had come on man when he lost contact with this harmony, and all of his thoughts and ways fell into disorder.

It was evident that means must be found to restore man's communion with the marvel. These were the *li*, the rites and ceremonies which, in miniature, recreated the perfect pattern by which Heaven's favor was attracted—not only the great rites of state and temple, but the small rites of private life—personal conduct, which we call manners and etiquette.

Because of his emphasis on *li*, particularly the old *li* that he had learned from old scholars and dug out of old books, Confucius has been accused of wanting to turn the clock back. This does not take into account his artistry, his tastefulness. How can an artist admit a difference between what is old-fashioned and what is new-fangled? There is only what is right. The effort of Confucius was to strip the *li* of the encrustations of time, so that their classic purity stood forth. He wished men to behave with good taste and good sense, because it was obvious to him that the way men behave, dress, and speak, whether in the reverential performance of some public ceremony or in the correct manners of intimate life, has a disciplinary effect, with consequences, both seen and unseen for his society.

The Master said, "The educational and transforming power of manners is most subtle. They check depravity before it has taken form. They cause a man daily to tend toward the good and keep him from wrongdoing without his even being conscious of it. That is why the ancient kings valued manners so highly."

"The *li* pierce the good will of spiritual intelligences. They bring down spirits from above. They lift up a soul that is abased."

"Listening to music brings harmony to the mind. Right conduct brings harmony to existence."

"If in your performance of a public ceremony you find yourself guilty of showing off, restrain yourself."

The Doctrine of the Mean

To realize his high lineage as a child of the Universe, and act upon it, was not only the individual's noblest aim; it was his duty to society. In the famous text called the *Chung Yung*, or the *Doctrine of the Mean*, it is written that a Path exists which can lead any man to his exact destiny—the purpose for which he, the individual, was born. Whether prince or peasant, rich or poor, barbarian or civilized man, he can only be perfectly happy so long as he is traveling toward his natural destiny.

Christ expressed this idea in poetic terms, pointing to the fowls of the air and the lilies of the field which are well-fed and splendidly clothed, just doing what they were created to do, artlessly obedient to the nature of things.

Indeed, the Path of Confucius is defined as nature—human nature. If man desires to find out Heaven's will, let him do it through knowing himself. "Heaven's purpose is contained in our nature."

Confucius leads one into the sanctuary of the self with mysterious words, almost as if he had detected the Freudian demons lurking there: "There is nothing more visible than what is unseen, nothing more obvious than what is very small."

Secret thoughts must be kept in check, extravagance curbed, weakness of character rooted out. Somewhere on the journey inward, beyond the dim corridors where emotions fuddle the wind, there is a quiet grove where one may rest. It is a point in the germ of being, a link with the whole universe. Here the will of Heaven becomes clear, the Path unfolds, well marked unto infinity. The ugly knock and clang of worldliness are stilled, replaced by the harmonious swing of creation.

The *Chung Yung* is the most mystical of the texts attributed to Confucius, and some modern students do not believe that the great humanist had anything to do with it. However, if we believe that the *Lun Yü*, the

Collected Sayings, are a direct expression of his thought, we must admit that Confucius believed in a Path which was at once spiritual and ethical, and which, if it was followed, brought one into harmonious action with nature.

Of the Path, the Master said:

"The Path is very near to men. When someone tries to follow a course of action unnatural to his thought, it is not the Path."

"The most ordinary man or woman may tread the Path, but it leads to realms where even the sage is a stranger."

"Archery shows us how to find the Path. When an archer misses his aim, he blames no one, but looks for the fault in himself."

"It is man who makes the Path great. It is not the Path that makes man great."

On Virtue

Virtue is man's natural inheritance. Furthermore, it is the key to the Path. Any individual can claim the glorious heirloom simply by reaching out and grasping the key. Confucius had a great many complaints about the behavior of men, but he never had the slightest doubt that man is good.

In following the Master's teaching, there are two ways of looking at virtue. First, one may view it as the essential magic with which all matter is imbued. Second, it can be regarded as a multitude of separate splendors, aspects of the human character which ought to be cultivated in the incubator of the self. He selected five of them for special praise: magnanimity, uprightness, sagacity, sincerity, and kindness. Loyalty, reliability, and a sense of justice were also to be cultivated.

The greatest of virtues was kindness. This was the source from which all others flowed—the goal, not only of the individual, but of all human institutions, such as the state. It was the whole reason for politics, the essence of education, the inner meaning of laws, rites, etiquette—*kindness.*

Well might the Master say, "Ah! to live only among the virtuous. I can imagine no happier fate."

"Lacking virtue, what good does it do to know the rules of conduct?"

"Those without virtue cannot face misfortune, but for the virtuous, virtue is its own reward."

"Be only partly virtuous; you will still find yourself incapable of an unkind deed."

"Virtue never lives alone. It attracts company."

"The thinking man loves water; the virtuous man loves mountains. That is because the thinking man's mind is active and ever-flowing, while the virtuous man's mind is

tranquil. The thinking man seeks enjoyment, the virtuous man simply enjoys."

Of Education

The spiritual teachers of ancient times had little to say
about earthly knowledge except to compare it unfavor-
ably with spiritual quality: "Though I . . . understand all
mysteries and all knowledge . . . and have not charity, I
am nothing," wrote Saint Paul to his congregation at
Corinth.

Confucius placed learning, the kind gained through
systematic education, close to the center of his teaching.
While advising, in the *Doctrine of the Mean,* inward-
looking self-examination as a means of arriving at truth,
he knew how hard it was and that for some people it was
impossible. He had tried it himself: "I have spent a day
and a night without eating or sleeping, in meditation.
It was no use. It is better to learn."

Confucius thought that education was a means of gaining an enlightened mind: not "enlightenment" in the
mystical sense, but the equivalent in an earthly sense,
when to the mentality disciplined and expanded by study,
the remarkable harmonies of nature would become plain.
One had to fill oneself with knowledge like a vessel. Upon
the knowledge gained, the indwelling truth would act
like a yeast, forcing the mind to assume its original
perfect shape: " . . . when their minds were cultivated,
their thoughts became pure."

He admitted that knowledge itself was arid and mean-
ingless: "Learning without thought is labor lost." But he

added a warning for self-made and self-styled philosophers: "Thought without learning is dangerous."

Confucius said:

"The ruler with a well-trained mind learns to love
the men he governs. As for those born to the common lot,
when their minds are trained, they accept government."

"A scholar, wishing to learn, but ashamed of his clothes!
I have nothing to say to him at all."

"When people are educated, the distinction between
classes disappears."

"Learn as if you could never have enough of learning,
as if you might miss something."

"To love virtue and not learning: a simpleton
To love knowing and not learning: shallowness
To love honesty and not learning: naïveté
To love plain speech and not learning: a boor
To love physical strength and not learning: a rebel
To love determination and not learning: recklessness."

"Without learning, the wise become foolish; by learning the foolish become wise."

On the Ruler

The higher a man's rank, the more urgent it was that
his feet should find the Path and his heart become illumi
nated by virtue. "When the ruler behaves himself cor-

rectly, the people will also." This was the instruction Confucius incessantly gave the princes. With the passionate conviction of the artist, he would have liked to take them between his giant hands and recreate them into the heroic shape of the sage-kings of old, whose radiating virtue, held all in its beam.

"Cherish the people," he exhorted the princes. "See that they have enough to eat. Honor the dead. Be kind so that people will turn to you. Be reliable, so that they will trust you. Be industrious, and you will achieve. Put public interest first, always."

They did not listen to him.

The Master told the rulers of his day:
"A ruler with faults should not object to changing them."

"A master should demand of his subordinates only what he has taught them."

"A governor should not concern himself with small achievements lest the important things never get done."

"A certain virtuous minister was raised to office three times without rejoicing, and he was removed from office three times, without resentment. He always told his successor everything he knew about the business of state."

"To gather in the wealth is to disperse the people. To distribute wealth is to attract the people."

"A state needs three things: sufficient food, sufficient military equipment, and the confidence of the people in their government."

"If you had to eliminate one, which would you give up first?"

"Military equipment."

"And next?"

"Food. Because everyone must die, and life is not worth much unless people have confidence in their government."

"I detest the sight of an unkind man ruling."

The ultimate ideal of Confucian thinking is *Ta Ting,* a world commonwealth. At United Nations headquarters in New York hangs a plaque of black marble, inscribed in gold in the Chinese calligraphy of Dr. Sun Yat-sen, the "father of the Chinese revolution." The quotation is from the *Li Chi,* the *Book of Rites.*

When the Great Principle prevails, the world is a commonwealth in which rulers are selected according to their wisdom and ability. Mutual confidence is promoted and good neighborliness cultivated. Hence, men do not regard as parents only their own parents, nor do they treat as children only their own children. Provision is secured for the aged until death, employment for the able-bodied, and the means of growing up for the young. Helpless widows and widowers, orphans and the lonely, as well as the sick and the disabled, are well cared for. Men have their respective occupations and women their homes. They do not like to see wealth lying idle, yet they do not keep it for their own gratification. They despise indolence, yet they do not use their energies for their own benefit. In this way, selfish schemings are repressed, and robbers, thieves and other lawless men no longer exist, and there is no need for people to shut their outer doors.

This is called the Great Harmony.

On the Family

The prince was the pivot around which well-regulated society turned. According to the *Great Learning,* his success as a statesman would depend upon his ability to regulate his family. The Master said, "The ceremony of marriage lies at the foundation of government."

All of the virtues so important to the cultivation of character were to be practiced first in the home. Loyalty, one of the paramount virtues, began between family members. Once someone told the Master, "Where I come from, people are very dependable. If a man were to steal a sheep, his own son would give him up."

Confucius was profoundly shocked. He replied, "Where I come from, people are also dependable. A son can depend upon his father and a father upon his son."

In the *Great Learning* it is written: "From the loving example of one family, love radiates through the state; its courtesies become the courtesies of society."

Confucius himself knew nothing of the delights of

normal family life; nevertheless his human observations sometimes bind the ancient and modern world with sudden lightening threads: "A father is proud of the ablest among his sons, but a mother, while she is proud of the ablest, cherishes the less able. A mother's pride is expressed in affection. A father's affection is expressed in pride."

The Master said:

"As a son, practice filial piety. As a father, practice kindness."

"A father should deal severely—but privately—with the faults of his son."

"Those who cannot properly teach their families are themselves unteachable."

On Filial Piety

The well-regulated family is based on the efforts of the individual, who, for his own sake and that of society in general, practices self-mastery. Training should begin in childhood with the practice of filial piety. In the *Hsiao Ching,* the text which describes this training, it is written, "The filial duty of a man toward his parents becomes loyalty to his prince; fraternal duty becomes loyalty to elders; family duty becomes duty to society."

The first principle of filial piety was not the abasement of the young before the old but the contrary—self-respect. "As the offshoot of his parents, how dare a child not respect himself?"

The doctrine of filial piety is perhaps the most famous of the teachings of Confucius and the one that has made the greatest impression on the Western world, possibly because some of the moral tales that grew up around it seem to be a curious Far Eastern way of saying, "Honor thy father and thy mother." We read with amusement of the young man who, when his stepmother expressed a desire to eat fish in midwinter, stripped himself naked and sat on the icy surface of a lake until he had melted a hole for the fish to jump through.

Confucius would surely have told that young man to put on his clothes. His pronouncements on the subject of filial piety are simple and humane, as always.

"Let your parents' only reason for worry be whether you are healthy."

"Your parents gave you bodies, hair, and skin, every bit of you. Take care of them."

"Nowadays filial piety seems to mean that a man just supports his parents—he does the same for his horses and dogs. Reverence of a parent is what distinguishes filial piety."

"While your parents are alive, don't go too far away from home, and wherever you go, always let them know where you are."

"Children should always know their parents' age. It

should be a source of joy to them as well as of apprehension."

The Superior Man

Confucius held the view that, when the state followed the Path, a man who followed the Path would automatically find a place of honor in it, but when the times were out of joint, he should recognize that in politics there was small room for him.

The governments of his time were certainly not open to honest or thoughtful criticism. Hardly any of the Master's surviving words are directed at persons or situations, like those, for example, of Cicero or Cato. Instead he spoke in terms of ideals: the ideal society, such as had existed in the Golden Age; the ideal prince, such as the sage-kings had been; the ideal minister, father, son; and embracing them all, the ideal man, the Superior Man. In this personification of human nature made perfect, the ideas of Confucius march through the misty years into our modern understanding.

The Superior Man is not a saint, nor is he an armchair statesman or an ivory-tower intellectual. He is social and political, a man who does business and knows affairs. In private life he is a noble-minded gentleman, in professional life a humble-minded public servant. He might be aristocrat or peasant; in the context of a moral society, his path will be inevitably upward, while that of the small-minded man is downward. One of the most radical teachings of Confucius was, "The sons of emperors and princes, if they are without quality, should be reduced to the rank of the common people; the sons of the common people, with quality, should be elevated to the class of rulers."

Such ideas, forming the basis of Confucian ethics, made it possible for many centuries for Chinese of all social degrees to become mandarins.

Confucius said, "Men are by nature very much alike. It is circumstances that draw them apart." This is, however, as close as he came to stating "the equality of man," a notion which, since it conflicts with everyday observation, was not typical of him. It seemed to him quite obvious that some people make the best of themselves, while others only "eat their fill and fix their minds on nothing." Nor was he blind to Nature's seeming injustices. He said, "The highest type of man is born with understanding; the next highest acquires understanding; the next highest seeks to understand as much as he can; and the lowest class of man does not grasp that there is anything to understand."

Yet, even drawing these lines, he did not leave foothold in his teaching for the formation of rigid social classes or castes. Once Tze Lu asked him, "What exactly makes a Superior Man?"

"Earnest and careful cultivation of himself," replied Confucius. As always, he placed responsibility for choosing a course of action squarely on the individual—provided his intelligence told him he had a choice.

We should not overlook the fact that there is another level, more poetic and romantic, on which we may understand the Superior Man. He is none other than the hero of the Master's boyhood, the irreproachable Duke of Chou. Deeper still, he is the "would-be" Confucius, the perfect image of himself, rising on the wings of a phoenix above the failures of his life.

Of course, he disclaimed any such grandeur. "I am not a Superior Man. I am only one who strives."

"The Superior Man loves quality; the small man loves comfort."

"The Superior Man gravely awaits the will of Heaven; the small man anxiously awaits a stroke of luck."

"The Superior Man lives by ruling his desires, the small man by getting special favors."

"The Superior Man is friendly, but he is not familiar; the small man is familiar, but he is quarrelsome more often than friendly."

"The Superior Man brings out the best in others; the small man does the opposite."

"The Superior Man is poised and at ease; the small man is self-conscious."

"The Superior Man thinks of what is right; the small man thinks of what is profitable."

"The Superior Man understands broad issues; the small man understands details. The Superior Man considers how much he can do; the small man considers how to do it."

"The Superior Man takes his lot calmly; the small man is full of complaints."

"The Superior Man is universal in outlook and impartial. The small man is partial, and therefore he cannot have a universal point of view."

"A Superior Man demands much of himself; a small man demands much of others."

"The Superior Man willingly helps others attain what he himself desires."

"When you see a Superior Man, imitate him; when you see a small man, compare yourself."

"The Superior Man does not belong to cliques."

"The Superior Man is nobody's tool."

"The Superior Man never expects to be cheated; but when he is being cheated, he is the first to perceive it."

"The Superior Man is superior even in haste, even in pain."

"A Superior Man does not compete. A sports contest is an exception; if he loses, he is still affable, still superior."

"A Superior Man is slow to talk but quick to act."

"A Superior Man is easy to serve but hard to please."

"The Superior Man is modest, generous, openhearted, industrious, and kind."

"The Superior Man is always himself. In a low position, he does not court favor; in a high position, he is not condescending. He is himself, and content to be so."

"The Superior Man dislikes those who advertise the faults of others, who slander their superiors, who are courageous without self-control, who are aggressive without thinking."

"The Superior Man is watchful of these things: his eyes, so that he may observe; his ears, that he may learn; his face, that it may reflect kindness always; his manners, that they might show respect for others; his words, that they may be true; his business dealings, that they may be fair; his doubts, that he may resolve them; his emotions, that he may control them; his money, that he may earn it honestly."

"Anybody can be a Superior Man. It is only necessary to decide to be one."

On a Number of Things

In the course of his long life, Confucius made a great many observations about people and things, and through his words the sharp-witted, thoughtful, and benevolent philosopher comes to life.

The Master said, "I am lucky. If I have faults, people are sure to notice them."

"The only real fault is not to change one's faults."

"I have never met a man who blamed himself for his faults."

"A man may have all qualities, but if he is conceited and stingy, he is without quality."

On modern music: "Why are they using an ax to kill that chicken when a hatchet would do as well?"

"There are three hundred *Odes,* but they can all be summed up in a single phrase: Think straight."

"People desire money and position; if these cannot be acquired honorably, they should be avoided. People fear poverty and obscurity; if these cannot be avoided honorably, they should be accepted."

"It is hard to be poor and not resent it. It is easy to be rich and well disposed."

"Knowing what one knows; knowing also what one does not know—this is knowledge."

"Simplicity is good. But to act simple when you are simple—really, that is too much simplicity."

"One who refuses to think about future problems will soon have them falling about his ears."

"In public, respect your superiors; at home, respect your parents and elders. Do not drink too much."

"Do not be stubborn. Do not be self-centered."

"Be considerate of your elders, openhearted with friends, and treat the young ones tenderly."

"Have no friends not equal to yourself."

"I am not disturbed that a man does not know of me, but it disturbs me not to know of him."

"Two kinds of men are unteachable: the very wise and the very stupid."

On Reciprocity

A constant interchange of virtue takes place between Heaven and Earth, gods and men, ruler and people, individual and family, family and society, and there is a net that holds them all together.

Once Tze Kung asked Confucius if there was one

word that embodied all his teaching. The Master replied, "Yes—'reciprocity.' "

He added then, by way of explanation—though he said it in a way we're unused to—the remarkable civilizing idea cherished by all of us:

"Do not do unto others that which you do not wish them to do unto you."

THE MASTER

11. *"At Sixty ..."*

"At sixty, I could bow to immovable truth."

A frequent question put to Confucius was, "What is the secret of good government?" Quite often he replied with one of his characteristic teachings: "Calling things by their right names." He was the inventor of the modern science of semantics.

Confucius regarded the names of things as an important tool of correct thinking. When words change meanings or acquire double meanings, they tend to mislead, divide, and confuse. Precise thoughts, particularly laws, can only be framed with precise words, he taught. "If names are not correct, the prince's judgments are not clear. If the prince's judgments are not clear, his laws are not carried out. If the laws are not carried out, tradition loses meaning. If tradition loses meaning, so does justice, and the people have nowhere to turn."

At the turn of the fifth century B.C., as the Spring and Autumn Period drew to its close, nothing could be called by its right name in the Chou kingdom, which was no kingdom but a tangle of warring provinces where vassals were rebels, governors were tyrants, and ministers of government were assassins and scoundrels. Justice, rites, and music did not flourish, nor any of the noble occupations humans proudly call the humanities.

In such perilous times, it is inevitable that many people simply detach themselves from normal attitudes of mind; they "drop out." Unable to make sense of the outer world, they turn to the eternal order that is said to exist in the secret chambers of the mind. Confucius turned inward, in a way, when he immersed himself in music. But essentially, he was a man of affairs, and his instinct was to tackle the practical problems of life in a practical manner.

However, we should remember that according to a tradition, when Confucius was a young man he had visited the royal city of Loyang, and there in the dim archives of the king's library he had met and conversed with the famous mystic, Lao-tze, the "Old Master." His philosophy, which taught the illusory nature of the world and its struggles, was having a profound influence upon the times. Lao-tze, according to the story, immediately discerned the ambition of his visitor, and he earnestly advised him to turn away from it and to direct his mind instead to the only reality, which was to be found in the spiritual realm.

"Those who are rich and great seem to know everything and own everything," said Lao-tze to Confucius. "But they only serve to illustrate human folly."

It was shortly after this conversation that Lao-tze got on his water buffalo and traveled westward toward the land of the barbarians, and he was never seen again. But he left behind him his teaching, the *Tao,* the mystic Way, and this, threaded with the thought of Confucius and Gautama Buddha, wove the great tapestry of China.

Whether or not this meeting took place, a series of traditions concerning the later years of Confucius suggests to us that the influence of the Taoists had not passed him by.

It was the year after Jan Ch'iu left the company of disciples that Confucius, while paying a visit to a certain nobleman, delivered one of his famous definitions of correct government: "The art of government consists in making people happy; in keeping one's own people at home and attracting those from abroad."

Later, the nobleman asked Tze Lu privately, "What sort of a man is Master K'ung?" When Tze Lu reported this question, the Master said, "You should have told him I am one who seeks truth without tiring and teaches mankind without getting disgusted. Also, I am so industrious that I forget to eat and never notice that I am getting old."

He had every reason to speak with weary irony; his life was becoming that of a perpetual refugee. The state of Ch'en, where he had lived contentedly for a while, was ground under by war. The household pulled up roots and settled down again, this time in the state of Ts'ai. But Ts'ai was soon caught up in a monstrous squabble involving several giant states, and again the sage and his company were obliged to remove themselves and wait until the heavy shadow of armed men had staggered away to another part of the realm.

They returned home across a countryside seared by war.

Nearing their destination and making for the river ford, they passed some men patiently digging the earth, undiscouraged by the desolation around them. At first sight they looked like poor farmers stolidly weeding and hoeing their patch beside the river, but something odd about them, perhaps their ascetic features and fine skin, prompted Confucius to remark, "They are not what they seem. They are mystics." They did not greet him, and so he stopped his chariot and sent Tze Lu to ask where the river could be crossed. "Who is this person?" one of the ascetics asked Tze Lu.

"It is Master K'ung," said Tze Lu.

"Master K'ung of Lu?"

"Yes."

"Well," said the ascetic drily, "in that case he must know all there is to know about crossing rivers."

Then the other ascetic said, "Are you one of his disciples?"

"Yes," said Tze Lu.

"The world is drowning in a flood of sorrow," said the ascetic. "What does your Master think he can do to change things? Instead of following a man who is always having to remove himself from difficulties, you ought to follow one who removes himself from the world."

He then turned away and went on digging. Tze Lu returned to the chariot and reported this conversation to Confucius, who replied with asperity, "Really! I cannot live with the birds and beasts. If order prevailed on earth, then of course I shouldn't want to change anything, should I?"

It seems that his residence was not far away from the colony of ascetics, for another day, when Confucius had been out walking for many hours, Tze Lu went to look for him and ran into another mystic. "Have you seen Master K'ung?" he asked.

The man looked Tze Lu up and down. "Your four limbs are not fit for work. You can't tell one kind of grain from another. You haven't got much of a Master, have you?" He thrust his staff into the ground and began to weed.

It is possible that during the three years Confucius lived in that spot, he might have conversed with these blunt-spoken hermits and have learned something of their philosophy.

In 489, fire and brimstone lowered again: the ministers of Ts'ai assassinated their Duke. To restore order, the huge, rich kingdom of Ch'u, to the south, sent an occupying force into the land.

The kingdom of Ch'u, mighty as it was at this time, had only in the previous century graduated from a rather primitive status. In earlier times, when the Chou Dynasty was at the height of power, the people of this area on the outskirts of the river valley had been outer barbarians, beyond the pale of polite society. Because of this, Ch'u felt inferior in culture to the central states. Therefore, when the King of Ch'u came with his army to Ts'ai, he was elated to be told that the most cultivated man in the world lived not too far away from his encampment. He immediately sent an invitation to Confucius to visit him. Etiquette demanded that Confucius pay him a visit, if only to thank him for the invitation, and so he set out upon the road.

This development did not please the distinguished assassins of Ts'ai. They did not want to take the advice of Confucius themselves, but they feared his advising a powerful neighbor. "Master K'ung is far too critical of faults," they said to each other, "and he has been living in these parts long enough to know the faults of every one of us. Now that the King of Ch'u has summoned him, he might well be offered a post in government. If he gains influence in Ch'u, who knows what he will say about us?"

Thereupon they sent out armed servants to intercept Confucius as he was on his way to the encampment of Ch'u. The sage and his companions were overtaken just as they were about to cross a field. The armed men, with rude shouts and menacing gestures, herded the little group together in the field and formed a circle around them with every seeming intention of camping there until the scholars starved to death. Confucius did not show fear. He sat down and began to discourse to his disciples. When he saw that their thoughts were wandering, he took out his lute and began to play to them and recite, with exquisite art, from the *Odes*. We are not told how many hours or even days this continued, but the company ran out of food and drink. Confucius remained calm, sometimes singing, otherwise sunk in meditation.

At length Tze Lu became impatient with this fortitude. "Aren't you hungry or thirsty at all?" he snapped. Confucius said, "The Superior Man remains firm in times of want; the inferior man gives way."

But Tze Kung also was weary of being brave; he wanted the Master to put down his lute and apply himself to a plan of escape. Confucius said, "Old friend, you probably think I know everything, don't you?"

"Well," replied Tze Kung. "It's true, isn't it?"

"No," said Confucius. "There is one thing left to know."

"What is that?"

"I seek the all-pervading unity."

These words, which voice the familiar yearning of the mystic, strongly suggest that Confucius had spent some time in the past three years in conversation with his near neighbors, the followers of the Tao, and that they had convinced him that great as his intellectual attainment was, he had yet to attain the transcendental knowledge that lies at the bottom of the mind, on the underside of reason.

And so, in the peril of the moment, he turned inward, seeking immovable truth. But it was an unnatural state of mind for him. Reason and logic had always been his guide and comfort, and now, as he sought to withdraw from hunger, thirst, and mortal fear, a memory of a verse from an ode intruded, and prodded him:

> "Are we rhinoceroses
>   Or tigers?
> To stay in this wilderness?"

Thus, his mind refused to escape the immediate problem and the tragedy that lay at the root of it—his utter personal failure. He called Tze Lu to him. "In theory," he said, "if my ideas were true, I would be successful, honored, powerful, acclaimed. Then no one would want to trap us here and starve us to death. Since they do, I suppose this means that my ideas are false. What do you think?"

As we know, Tze Lu was an honest conservative who feared that in some ways Confucius was a menace to the established order. He was too loving a friend to lay blame on his Master; he simply spoke of himself: "Certainly I cannot have attained true goodness or true wisdom, for people do not trust me or listen to anything I say."

"Perhaps you are right," said Confucius heavily. "And yet, you are wrong, because how do you explain all the truly great men who have met with misfortune? If good philosophers were automatically honored, none of them would ever have a care. But history tells us that this is far from the case."

He brought up the same doubts to Tze Kung. "Is my teaching false?" he asked. "Is that why we are not powerful and successful and why we are sitting in this field?"

Tze Kung was the most eloquent of the disciples, famous for his gift of persuasive speech. He exclaimed loyally, "No, no! Of course your teachings are not false. If they are to be criticized at all, it is just that they are a little highbrow. They go over people's heads. Perhaps if you brought them closer to the understanding of ordinary people . . ."

Confucius said, "Dear friend, a farmer sows, but he doesn't make the harvest. A workman may do skillful work, but if his style does not strike the fancy of his times, he will fail. I can sift and organize and simplify and over-simplify until I die but if minds are not ripe to be taught, I shall still not be listened to. No, that is not the answer."

Next the Master spoke to his favorite pupil, Yen Hui. "Why are we in such trouble, my son?" he asked. "Is there something wrong with my teaching?"

"Your teaching is the truth, Master," replied Yen Hui firmly. Then he continued, "However, people don't recognize the truth at first. If they did, they would have no choice but to live by it. We recognize it, and we live by it. Our rulers do not, and so they live in error.

"Still, what does it matter whether anyone recognizes your teachings now or not? Truth endures; in the end it prevails. In a way, the fact that people find your teaching hard to accept is a recognition of it."

Yen Hui was like this—simple and subtle, gentle and yet penetrating. Confucius was greatly cheered. Smiling, he said, "Son of the house of Yen, if you were a rich lord, I'd want to be your overseer."

In the end, it was Tze Kung who rescued them from their predicament, by smuggling himself by night through the enemy lines. He swiftly made his way to the encampment of the King of Ch'u, who sent a military escort to beat off the besiegers and lead the company to the safety of his camp.

As it turned out, the dignitaries of Ts'ai had been absolutely right. The King had every intention of making Confucius a present of a fief of seven hundred square miles. What great things Confucius would have done with this princely gift can only be guessed. However, while he had been trapped in the field, the King's advisers had been planning a defense against this rival.

The prime minister, in particular, demonstrated an advanced grasp of diplomatic technique, even if his grandfather had been a common barbarian jumping about with bones in his hair. He asked the King: "Your Majesty, among all your diplomats, is there one who is the equal of the Master's disciple, Tze Kung?"

"No," said the King.

"And among your generals, is any the equal of Tze Lu?"

"No," said the King.

"And among your advisers, is any as wise as Yen Hui?"

"No," said the King.

"Then, sir, consider this: King Wen and King Wu started with only a hundred square miles, and finally they ruled the world. Do you think that bestowing seven hundred square miles on Confucius, who has the learning of three dynasties behind him and all those excellent advisers to help him, will turn out to the advantage of Ch'u?"

"No," said the King.

The King of Ch'u entertained Confucius royally, but he kept his fief in his pocket. Once, when Confucius was driving around the encampment in his chariot, the King's court jester passed him and sang him a little song, half jeering and half sympathetic:

> "O phoenix-bird, O phoenix-bird!
> Your splendor's gone—
> But what's done's done!
>
> Don't try so hard, don't fly so high:
> These days the ride
> Is suicide."

12. "A Bird Can Seek a Tree . . ."

"A bird can seek a tree,
but a tree cannot seek a bird."

After leaving the King's encampment, the Master re-treated back to the home of his hospitable friends in Wei, and from there he watched the political affairs of the central states proceed to wrack and ruin. After the Spring and Autumn Period there would follow the Period of the Warring States, and these few decades of utter confusion were already gaining momentum. In Lu, the new ruler, Duke Ai, was knee-deep in quarrels with neighboring states, and he was looking around for a master diplomat to help him out of them. The cleverest diplomat of all was Tze Kung, and Duke Ai called him home to Lu.

Possibly Confucius was hurt to see his old friend pre-ferred over himself, but he hid his feelings and sent him off with benign advice that showed how the years had sweetened his regard for the state of Wei: "Remember that the governments of Lu and Wei are brothers."

Tze Kung was able to smooth over the Duke's difficul-ties. Apart from his own skill and persuasiveness, there was another reason why he was able to do this. By this time the governments of most states contained men who had been disciples of Confucius. The Master was a failure, but his pupils were great men, and through them his unifying influence was secretly at work among the squabbling clans of the Yellow River Valley.

It was now eight years since Jan Ch'iu had gone home to serve the Chi family as steward, and he had done nothing to obtain the recall of his Master. Jan Ch'iu was always a slow and cautious man. Then, in 484, he won distinguished fame. Placed in command of the army, he not only repulsed the invading force but chased the enemy home, not forgetting to take possession of a large and rich slice of their territory. His master, Baron K'ang, said to him in amazement, "Do you come by your military skill naturally, or have you learned it from someone?"

Now Jan Ch'iu, although falling short of the Master's ideal pupil, shared the genuine affection that most of the disciples had for him. Perhaps he was not telling the truth, but he seized this golden opportunity to say, "I learned military skill from Master K'ung."

It was the very thing to ignite the Baron's interest. "What sort of man is this Master K'ung?" he wanted to know.

Jan Ch'iu replied: "If you call him home, you will never regret it. Ask anyone. Ask the diviners in the temple if you like—they'll all tell you that Confucius is a man of honor. Lands! Fiefs! You could give him a thousand square miles, and he'd never count the value of it, so long as honor was at stake."

The Baron said, "I'd like to summon him if you think he would come."

"Summon him," said Jan Ch'iu, and then he added, "But remember you must never let him be undermined by inferior people."

At that time, Confucius had, for a change, a job. He was serving, or trying to serve, as administrative adviser to the regent of Wei. This person, an upstart, had stepped forward in the confusion that followed the death of the old Duke and had made himself master of the country by three clever moves: first by marrying a princess of Wei, second by marrying his daughters to princes of Wei, and third by persuading Confucius to be his chief adviser in government.

Confucius tried hard to believe the best of this regent; it was only through this ruthless man of power that anyone could hope to influence affairs and perhaps coax life into the dark and smoldering landscape. But it was a lion-and-lamb relationship from the start. As time went by, the regent's quarrels with the royal family and with his in-laws overwhelmed and paralyzed all governmental activities. Confucius found himself asked to deliver advice that had nothing to do with governing a state, only to keeping the regent in power.

Finally he had had enough. When he was called upon to help plan a military campaign against one of the regent's grumbling sons-in-law, Confucius refused. He reiterated for the hundredth time that he really knew nothing whatsoever about military matters; then he withdrew. Returning to his home, he called for his chariot to be harnessed and made ready once again to leave Wei. As he mounted his chariot, he said sadly and tiredly, "A bird can seek a tree for itself, but a tree cannot seek a bird."

And then, in this dark mood, he had the sudden joy of seeing that trees do, after all, stretch out their long arms for birds. For ahead of him on the road, coming from the direction of Lu, he saw a gorgeous convoy of chariots with colored ribbons painting the breeze behind them, and in the foremost chariots rode three great lords of Lu. Upon approaching Confucius, the noblemen dismounted and took in their arms three rolls of richly embroidered silk. Approaching with many a ceremonial bow, they placed these gifts before him and delivered the Duke's command: Master K'ung was to return at once to Lu.

Confucius was in his sixty-ninth year when he was recalled home, and he had been absent for fourteen years. Though some of the most influential men of his time addressed him as Master, he had no rank beyond that which he had inherited from his father. Now, it was a stroke of luck that Baron K'ang was disposed to admire Confucius. It was not that he thought that government was intended to make people happy—far from it. He was a practical man who possessed a huge treasure house full of grain, and a conscience the size of the least mouse in his treasure house.

But he had heard so much about Confucius. Over the years, the sophisticated people of his generation had come to appreciate the Master; it was the fashion to admire Confucius. He was becoming something of a living monument, and both Baron K'ang and Duke Ai had suddenly realized his value in terms of prestige to the state of Lu; by sending him presents of rich silk, they meant to advertise the fact that they, at least, were cultured enough to know a great man when they saw one and to offer him a worthy position at his home court.

Therefore, when Confucius arrived, Baron K'ang received him at once in audience, and went straight to the point. He began to describe his many burdens as a servant of the state, and said how difficult it was to find honest men to assist him.

Confucius replied, "Be honest yourself. Then those who serve you would not steal if you paid them."

Baron K'ang tried again. The times were to blame, he complained; everyone was bent upon his own gain. Confucius said, "Put straight men above the crooked, and all will become straight. Put crooked men above straight ones, and all will become crooked."

Such remarks to the topmost official in Lu showed how little of Tze Kung's diplomatic skill had rubbed off on the Master during their years in exile. His interview with Duke Ai went off in the same prickly fashion. The Duke asked the classic question: "What is the secret of good government?"

Confucius said, "Choosing the right officials."

We need go no further to guess why Baron K'ang changed his mind about elevating Confucius to a dignified position. It was no doubt this ugly honesty of the sage that all his years had stood in his way—that ingrained, proud nature of the upright man that all the polish and all the punishment in the world and all the good advice of friends can never change.

Yet it was noted that this new and final failure did not trouble Confucius as all the other failures had done. A change had come over him in the seventh decade of his

life. Ambition had evaporated. Some have seen in this
mellowness additional proof that he had been profoundly
affected by the opinions of his recent neighbors, the Tao-
ist mystics. It is possible, though, that he was just getting
old and tired, and well content to be home again, without
the buttons and pompons of office being affixed to his
bonnet.

That Confucius could never really detach himself from
the affairs of this world was proved by an incident that
happened soon after his homecoming. Baron K'ang had
ordered his steward, Jan Ch'iu, to devise a new scheme for
increasing the taxes of the farmers, though they had been
suffering hardship from the recent war. Jan Ch'iu was
dense enough to ask the Master's help. With unaccustomed
rage, Confucius rose up and denounced him before all the
company. He expelled Jan Ch'iu from the roll of his
friendship, calling to all the disciples, "He is no disciple
of mine! Beat your drums against him, come, my sons!
Drive him out of the house!"

The tax was levied. Nevertheless, the quarrel with Jan
Ch'iu was later rectified, and he was again admitted to the
circle. Confucius had once said, "To hide one's feelings
and pretend friendship with those for whom one feels
none—I'd be ashamed of such conduct." It is possible,
therefore, that Confucius' indignation had brought about
some softening or compromise in the matter of taxes.
Whatever was the case, it seems that Confucius was not
capable of bearing enmity toward one of his pupils, no
matter how much he disapproved of his policies.

It is a sign of the Master's uniqueness, not only that he
did not harbor enmity, but that the great men whom he

so pointedly criticized rarely bore grudges toward him. Possibly in the depths of their minds they understood that his ideas transcended the times, involving social paradoxes that statesmen of a later day would have to solve. Baron K'ang never ceased to admire Confucius and to patronize him, and he probably supported him financially. He often asked for his advice, although he rarely took it. How could he? "The aim of politics is to uphold the right," Confucius told him. "Lead people by doing right. Then no one else will do otherwise."

"Well, what do you say to criminal punishment—to killing the bad for the sake of the good?"

"Sir, why kill anyone? Show that your goal is good, and people will follow you. A ruler is to his subjects as the wind to the grass—the grass bends when the wind blows across it."

Perhaps the real reason Baron K'ang continued to come back for more of this sort of medicine is that in growing old, Confucius had learned to curb his temper and rarely spoke in anger. Like the sage-kings of old, he had extended his knowledge so far that he was beginning to grasp the nature of things, to sense the grandeur of faulty man who struggles endlessly to fashion Heaven out of earth.

In his old age, the burden of bitterness he had carried from childhood lifted from his heart. He settled down in an establishment of modest comfort, and from far and wide the young men came, and old ones too, to learn from him and be warmed by his wit, his tolerance, and his charm. By this time, he was by far the most famous of the black-haired people.

13. *"Not to Learn . . ."*

"Not to learn,
not to be able to talk about what one has learned,
not to be the better through having learned,
not to be able to change things towards the good—
all this would seem terribly sad to me."

Once a youth visiting Lu from abroad said sarcastically: "Great indeed is Confucius! He knows all sorts of things, but he hasn't made a name for himself in any of them."

By this time Confucius was used to such barbs, aimed at his lack of official position, and he was able to turn this one off with a joke. "Now how shall I make a name for myself? As an archer? A charioteer? I suppose I had better be a charioteer."

But the opening words of this rude jibe are among the most famous in the world, the text of countless scrolls that have hung (and still hang) on the study walls of Confucian scholars: *Great indeed is Confucius!*

By the time he was old, surely Confucius must have known that he was very great; that he had invented a new profession which he had been practicing superbly all his life, that of a teacher—not an ordinary teacher, an old clerk haphazardly guiding children in their letters and numbers, but a professor of education, one who purposefully collects the tools of thought that have been shaped in the past and hands them down for the young to use or to pass on in their turn. "I do not create. I transmit," he said. Then, as was his habit when he seemed to be taking himself too seriously, he added with irony, "I'm like old P'eng—always rambling on about the good old days."

But old P'eng, a well-known historian, was only a recorder. Confucius creatively redesigned what he transmitted, and he said, "If by studying the past a man learns to understand the present—only then is he fit to be a teacher."

Confucius was a person like Socrates, whom we can hardly imagine except in conversation, surrounded by disciples. We do not know how many men he taught—some have said there were three thousand of them; another tradition counts only seventy-two. We might assume that over a period of five decades, some hundreds of young men were attracted to the renowned scholar, who was immensely intelligent, learned, and also kind to the young, for he admonished: "A young person should be treated with the utmost respect. Some day he may be your equal, or your superior."

His course of study was three years. The Master complained, "It is hard to find anyone willing to study three years before earning material reward." Not that he had no respect for money. He reproved a rich pupil who had refused his salary from the state: "It would have been better to take it and share it with your acquaintances."

As a political theoretician, he had a sensible and very modern notion that for great masses of people, material needs were paramount: "What would you do first for the people if you could?" Jan Ch'iu once asked him.

"Make them rich," said the Master.

"And what then?"

"Then I would teach them."

This humane viewpoint belonged to a man who personally placed learning far above profit. "The Master rarely mentioned money." Was a thing moral? Was it useful? These matters interested him. He took his pupils from every class, without the slightest regard for their ability to pay for their tuition. "I shall always teach a man who wants to learn, no matter how little he offers me."

However, he did not waste his generosity. "I do not teach those who are not interested. If I explain one corner of a subject, I expect a pupil to grasp the other three himself, and if he does not, I let him go."

He made himself approachable to all who wished to see him. He reproved his disciples for wishing to prevent him from sitting down to talk with a certain young man. "When someone gets himself washed and dressed to come to see me," he declared, "I shall certainly see him." He added, "After all, I don't have to adopt him, do I?"

Interest on the part of another would instantly ignite his own enthusiasm, stirring the deep wells of his learning. "Sometimes I'm astonished by how much I know. When someone asks me a question, even a completely uneducated and ignorant person, I find myself pouring forth complete information, from beginning to end, until I wear the subject out."

He said, "I wasn't born knowing all I do. I acquired knowledge by working at it."

He taught the liberal arts. When an official came to him to learn something about agriculture, Confucius told him, "You had better find a farmer to teach you." Perhaps the man belatedly remembered that Confucius had been born a "son of Tsou," a mere villager. He tried to cover his mistake by saying that he really wanted to learn the gentler art of gardening. "Then find a gardener," said the Master testily.

Confucius accepted rustic boys as pupils, but he treated them as gentlemen and obliged them to live up to this treatment, not letting them go forth from his house with unpolished manners to face the scorn of the comfortably born, as he had done. Still, it was not the hollow motions of good breeding, but self-cultivation that he emphasized, including improvement of the personality, ethics, and moral qualities—the qualities of the Superior Man.

His textbooks were the *Odes,* the *History,* and all that was recorded of the doings and sayings of the sage-kings of old. A study of the *Rites and Ceremonies* was certainly part of the curriculum. Confucius was notable among ancient teachers in that he did not place excessive emphasis upon learning by rote. "Suppose a man can recite all the *Odes,*" he said, "and suppose he is on a mission of state; and then at a critical moment, it turns out that he doesn't know how to think. He may know the *Odes,* but he is not much use as a diplomat."

Confucius had observed that too much attention to sports, especially competitive sports, was likely to subtract from scholarly enthusiasm, and so, in the everyday life of his school, he preferred that they not be spoken of. He believed, too, that speculations about gods, fate, ghosts, and psychic marvels can engross youthful minds to the detriment of study, and so he would rarely allow such subjects to be introduced into the conversations. He was not mundane or agnostic, but he clearly saw that discussion of misty subjects did not make it easier to train young minds to think logically and exactly.

It was Confucius' way to strike a balance in all matters. He himself adored old things and old customs; yet "the Master taught by means of current events." His method of instruction seems to have been that of the best modern teaching—thorough discussion. The pupils read, or they observed; they pondered; they formed opinions. Then, individually or in groups, they discussed their thoughts with their Master, who acted at the same time the role of questioner and elicitor of thought, as well as the imparter of knowledge. By discussion he sharpened wits and deepened and broadened mental capacities. He liked his pupils to reciprocate. He complained jokingly about Yen Hui: "Much good he is—agreeing with everything I say."

A number of traditions demonstrate the careful regard the Master had for the individual character of his pupils. Once Tze Lu, who was at that time employed by Baron K'ang in a high position, became enthusiastic about a certain administrative scheme and wanted to put it into practice. "Don't do it before you have talked the matter

over with your father and elder brother," counseled the
sage. But to Jan Ch'iu, who also wanted to try out the
same idea, he said, "Yes, do so. Do it now."

A disciple who had heard both conversations confessed
himself puzzled. The Master explained: "Jan Ch'iu takes
an age to start anything, and so I hurried him up. Tze
Lu is too impulsive, and so I held him back."

None of the early traditions glorify or sanctify these
disciples or present them as model pupils; they were
human beings with faults and foibles that are preserved
in anecdotes. Of one young man the Master said, "I used
to listen to what men said and assume that their deeds
matched their words. Life with Tsai Yu has taught me to
listen to the words, and then watch carefully whether the
deeds match them."

It pleased him when one pupil, assessing his own
faults, refused a good post "because I am not yet ready
for it."

From such anecdotes the characters of the disciples
bloom forth for us. Tze Kung was too critical. "As for me,"
the Master told him, "not having yet made myself
perfect, I have no time to criticize others." Jan Ch'iu was
calculating. "Well, at least he wouldn't kill his father or
his prince."

Of his best friend, Tze Lu, the Master told Baron K'ang,
"He acts without thinking, and you will thus find him a
perfect politician."

In fact, Tze Lu became one of the most respected
statesmen of his time. He was so trusted, that foreign
diplomats, negotiating with Lu, far preferred his simple

spoken word to a treaty signed by Duke Ai. "Such an honest man will never die a natural death," the Master used to tease him.

Yen Hui, the favorite, lived in the shadow of his Master. He came from a poor family; once he had lived in an alley and had not had enough to eat, though no one had ever heard him complain. He sought no public office, nor did anyone offer him any, he was so modest and still.

Confucius considered him far wiser than himself. Yen Hui never got angry; he never made the same mistake twice, and never returned a slight; he treated inferiors as if they were superiors, and he rejoiced in the company of old friends as he did in that of new ones. His excellence was such that the Master said that Yen Hui was the only man he knew who could remain excellent for three solid months without a break; other disciples could manage only a month, and some of them only a day.

He was admired and loved by his fellow disciples. One of them said of him, "He could be entrusted with the rule of a state. He could be entrusted with the education of a young child."

The Master looked upon Yen Hui as his successor, who would carry on his work of teaching after he was gone. He sometimes expressed wonder that Yen Hui absorbed his ideas so completely that he never disagreed with anything he said, as the others did. "It makes him look stupid," he said, "as if he didn't understand. But he is not stupid. When I question him, I find that he *is* my teaching."

This procession of young men emerged from under the wings of the Master at the very beginning of China's history, and they spread over the Yellow River Valley as administrators, gentlemen, scholars, and teachers, professing, defending, and transmitting certain modes of behavior and attitudes of mind. It is pleasant to read about Tsai Yu who, when he was governor of a town, opened a public school for the common people where he personally taught them court manners, music, and the *Odes;* and of Tzeng Tze, one of the most important transmitters of the doctrine, who said, "Every day I ask myself three questions: Have I helped others? Have I been a true friend? Have I passed on what I was taught?"

They were proud of their Master, of their teaching, and of their cultivated minds. They spoke forthrightly to princes, as Confucius had shown them how to do. Yu Jo was consulted by the ever-needy Duke Ai: "What can we do when the harvest fails, and we haven't anything left in the treasury?"

"Levy a tax of one tenth."

"One tenth! I already levy a tax of two tenths and it isn't enough."

"When the people have plenty, how can the ruler fail to have enough? When the people are needy, how can the ruler bear to have enough?"

14. *"At Seventy . . ."*

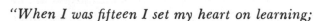

"When I was fifteen I set my heart on learning;
"At thirty I could stand on my own feet;
"At forty, I knew exactly where I was going;
"At fifty, I realized that Heaven had a will of its own;
"At sixty I could bow to immovable truth;
"At seventy I could follow my heart's desire
and never transgress what is right."

The words of Confucius that appear at the head of this chapter are almost an ode to the intellectual way of life. Countless scholars of every age and place must have quietly followed this road to its satisfying end. Confucius, when he was young, had identified his ideals with the excellent Duke of Chou. During his wandering years, when he saw himself excluded from life's grand design, he had looked anxiously for some sign from Heaven to give him hope, but Heaven gave none, and he cried out in despair: "No phoenix has appeared; nothing is to be read in the river swirls. This means no wise prince is destined to arise and bestride the age. Ah, no one needs me! I'm no use at all!"

Then he got old. No longer the prisoner of his ideals,

he was the personification of them. "I must be going into a decline," he said one day. "It is so long since I had a dream about the Duke of Chou."

It is strange that more is known about the private lives of mystical teachers such as Jesus Christ and Gautama Buddha than of Confucius, who was a man of the world. His wife is simply not mentioned in the traditions; probably he was a widower. At some time he seems to have become the head of the family of his handicapped elder half-brother, since we are told that he selected one of his own disciples as the husband of his niece.

He gave his daughter in marriage to a disciple who had been in prison, but Confucius considered that he would nevertheless make a good husband.

His son, First Carp, or Po Yu, as he is properly called, became his disciple, although probably not by choice. This young man was not cut out for the scholarly life, and it must have been crushing for him to be the son of a great scholar—especially one who set store on filial piety. A rather painful glimpse of the relations between father and son is recorded. Once, when expounding the virtues of the Odes, the Master turned to Po Yu and said, "Have you learned the first two sections?" When Po Yu said he had not, Confucius said, "Then you are like a man standing with his face against the wall."

Quite another sort of person was Po Yu's son, Tze Sse, who inherited his grandfather's tastes, and became a diligent and creative Confucian scholar.

The Master's pupils were his sons, and he called them so. In their company he spent the twilight years of his life, occupying his time with teaching and with various literary and musical labors. He is said to have given a very thorough overhauling to the *Shu Ching,* the *History,* sifting the records of a thousand years back, no doubt incorporating into them much of the mass of information he had collected during his long life and years of wandering. He is supposed to have edited the *Annals* of the Spring and Autumn Period, a history of events in the state of Lu beginning about 700 B.C. and continuing into the reign of his contemporary, Duke Ai.

He collected and selected the current traditions of the rites and ceremonies of the three dynasties that had gone before him, the Chou, the Yin, and the Hsia. He deeply studied the ancient music which accompanied the ceremonies. "Music is the inner motion of the soul, ceremony is the outer motion of the body. Let the outer motions be short and few, but let the music ring forth freely."

Like most old people, Confucius was discontented with the popular music of the day. "Music! They call it music! Are bells and drums all that is meant by music?" He felt strongly that since music has a powerful effect upon the feelings, only harmonious music, arousing the senses in a desirable direction, should be played. Upon his return from exile, he had found the music of Lu in dreadful state of disarray. "Music is one thing, sound another," he found reason to expostulate. "They are related, but they are not at all the same."

Now he had time to right this wrong. He set to work revising and rearranging the music of Lu, along with the editing of the *Odes,* or *Shih Ching.* He is said to have compiled this classic, selecting from three thousand poems, eliminating repetitions and adding new songs of literary merit. Whenever he heard someone singing a song he didn't know, he would want to hear it again and again, while he joined with his own voice; in this way, he prob-ably preserved many ancient songs from extinction. His musical notations have long since been lost, but the *Odes* themselves remain to us.

The work that is said to have absorbed him at this time was his commentary to the *I Ching,* the *Book of Changes,* the mysterious tome which in his youth, before he knew that Heaven had a will of its own, he had neglected. Now he became engrossed in the cryptic inter-change between the will of Heaven and the patterns of sticks thrown on the ground. He immersed himself in this ancient book, and he said, "Give me fifty more years of life to study the book called the *Changes,* and I shall perhaps get rid of all my faults."

Great, indeed, was Confucius in those last years, an object of curiosity to all of his people. When he went out in his field to practice archery, the crowds that gathered to watch him formed a solid wall. It was elegance of style, not skill at hitting a target, that mattered, he used to say.

When he was indisposed, the great Baron K'ang himself sent him a medicine, but the Master said suspiciously, "Not knowing what he's put in it, I'm not going to taste it." Duke Ai came to visit him as he lay ill. On such occa-sions, Confucius would have his court robes laid over him, sash and bows correctly placed across the portly mound, so that by only a slight feat of imagination, the Duke would see him upright and impeccably clad.

Whatever he said now was treasured and remembered. Age was softening the gravity of his pronouncements, and he was prone to smile at his own teaching. Once he listened to some disciples playing their favorite game—planning what they would do if they had an entire state at their disposal. One wanted to arm it to the teeth; another wanted to make it rich; another wanted the rites and ceremonies to be conducted in a certain way. The Master turned to a young disciple who was strumming his zither in the doorway. "What would you do, Tseng Tien?"

Tseng Tien, all in his good time, finished the melody, put down his zither, and said: "Well, in the spring when I put off my winter clothing, I'd go down to the river with other young men and bathe; and then I'd do a rain dance and go home singing."

Confucius laughed and said, "I am with you, Tseng Tien."

Meanwhile, around him, the lands of Chou continued to suffer under the rule of abominable people. In Wei, a family tussle began between a father and son disputing the throne. In Ch'i, where Confucius' old friend and enemy, Duke Ching, had died several years before, there was a sordid scandal. Duke Ching's heir, who was a small boy, was murdered by one of the infamous feudal families that dominated the land. A new duke was set up, but he too failed to please the powerful family, and he too was murdered. His son acceded to the throne. He rebeled and was murdered. These crimes took place one after the other in 481 B.C.

After the third assassination, Confucius fasted; then he bathed both head and body and donned his robes of state. He went to the court and asked for an audience with Duke Ai. Confucius then proposed to the Duke that Lu invade Ch'i at once and put an end to the murders.

"The fact is," replied the Duke, "we are weak, mostly because Ch'i has kept us weak for years. What could we possibly accomplish by an invasion?"

Confucius said, "The people of Ch'i are horrified by these assassinations; half of them would fight on our side. Add to them the army of Lu, and we could subdue Ch'i."

"Well," said the Duke, "go and talk to the lords of the Three Families. They manage everything in our state."

Confucius was dumbfounded by this lackadaisical attitude. With icy dignity he replied, "I am a knight and the son of a knight. In this moment of decision, I was bound by the rites to advise a course of action to your Highness. And now you say to me: 'Go and tell the three lords.' "

In spite of his indignation, the matter seemed serious enough that he swallowed his pride; he did present his plan to the three lords. But he had little hope that the feudal families of Lu would move against their counterparts in Ch'i. Indeed, the affair came to nothing. It was the last time Confucius tried to influence the destiny of nations.

Po Yu died, and Confucius mourned his son according

to his means, burying him in the way he felt the son of a scholar should be buried, in a simple coffin made of a single layer of wood.

Shortly afterward, calamity befell: Yen Hui died. The favorite, whom he had counted on to take his place when he was gone, was snatched from him by sudden illness. Confucius was thrown into the depths of despondency. Conventional rules of mourning, the dignity to be observed in the face of death's robberies, were thrown to the winds, and the Master wept without cease, crying, "Heaven is destroying me!" A disciple remonstrated, fearing that he was wasting his strength with excessive grief, and the Master replied with rare unkindness: "Too much grief! If I did not grieve for Yen Hui, for whom should I grieve?"

Into his sorrow there intruded Yen Hui's father, a simple, poor man who had undoubtedly rejoiced for years that his brilliant son had attained so glamorous a place at the right hand of a celebrated scholar. He could not understand why Confucius, who called Yen Hui "son," did not follow the spendthrift custom of the great and provide a magnificent, showy funeral, at which he, the true father, might look forward to playing a star role. Instead, Confucius had ordered, as he had done for Po Yu, a single-walled coffin. "You see, I call all my pupils sons," he explained to the old man, "regardless of whether they are brilliant or not. When my own son died, I buried him in a single-walled coffin, for that is all I can afford."

The old man's eyes wandered suspiciously down the wide veranda, to the pleasant garden, where the Master's oxcart stood with its brightly painted wheels.

"You could sell your chariot," he said.

The Master was greatly depressed at his inability to explain to this poor man the modest habits proper to a scholar.

However, the same subject was agitating the hearts of the disciples, some of whom were rich. Very likely they had let economy have its way with Po Yu, who was not truly a member of the group, but most of them had looked upon Yen Hui as the future leader of their school, and they felt he should have a double-walled coffin. They contributed to a pool which provided their dead colleague with a funeral that was all his father could have desired. But Confucius rebuked them. "Yen Hui thought of me as a father, and I wanted to treat him as I did my own son. But you would not let me. I am not pleased, my sons."

His sorrow for Yen Hui and his inability to affect the destiny of the state of Lu robbed Confucius of some of the serenity he had achieved during his last years. He began to fret again: "Alas, no one knows me."

"What do you mean, no one knows you?" Tze Kung asked him.

"Oh, I don't blame anyone. I stick to my studies and fix my mind on Heaven. At least Heaven knows me," he added morosely. He told Tze Kung a story about some wise men of old who were able to achieve detachment from the corrupt world. "But I am not like them," he said. "No, no. I suffer because I must leave the world without anyone knowing my name. How shall posterity ever remember me?"

It was not long after this conversation that he completed

the *Spring and Autumn Annals,* and when he had seen his work properly bound into slatted volumes, he handed them over to his pupils, saying, "If in future generations anyone recognizes me, it will be because of the *Annals.* And if anyone condemns me, it will be because of them."

As time is measured in history books, the Spring and Autumn Period came to an end on the day that Confucius closed his *Annals.* The Period of the Warring States had now begun. The year was 481 B.C.

In the spring, Duke Ai was accustomed to conduct a royal hunt in the great wilderness that lay in the western part of the state. In the hunt of 481, a strange beast was slain of a kind no one recognized. Carefully, they laid it in a wagon and bore it to Confucius, who looked at it and said, "It is a *ch'i lin.*"

The *ch'i lin,* which some say was the fabulous unicorn, was an animal seen so rarely that most people thought it was a myth; and when it came, who could tell whether it boded good or evil? A *ch'i lin* was said to have been seen in the vicinity of Tsou just before Confucius was born; now he brooded, certain that he knew what this prodigy meant. "My career is at an end," he said.

He took to his bed, and utterly miserable to leave the fascinating indifferent world, prepared for his last sleep. Dozing, he sensed a swish and murmur about his couch, and he opened his eyes to see Tze Lu and a large number of his disciples and important followers, arrayed in the stiff, silken garments of the high offices they held as ministers of state, diplomats, ambassadors, high chief stewards, governors of towns, commandants of fortresses.

He might have been a dying duke, or the King of Chou himself at Loyang. He was absolutely furious. He had spent his whole life trying to teach them all to call things by their right names, and before the breath was out of his body, here they were, busy playing grand games around his couch! "Whom do you think I am going to deceive, dying with all these ministers following me to my grave?" he boomed. "Heaven? Shall I deceive Heaven?" Then he added weakly, "Besides, isn't it better to die with you, my friends, than with a lot of ministers?"

He rallied from his weakness; in fact, it was Tze Lu who died the following year—just as the Master had predicted, by violent death owing to his own honesty. He held high office at the time, under the regent of Wei. When rebellion broke out, other vassals of the minister fled, but Tze Lu said, "I have eaten his pay, and I'll not run from his misfortune." He was killed battling the rebels.

One year after Tze Lu's death, in 479, Confucius, who was seventy-two years old, was walking back and forth in his courtyard, awaiting a visit from Tze Kung. The Master was ill and rather querulous. Although he knew that Kung was a busy man, he felt he had not come fast enough in response to his summons. "Why are you so late?" he said.

While waiting, he had recalled the sacred mountain Ch'iu Ni, after which he had received his personal name, and had made up a gloomy ditty. He sang it to Tze Kung:

> "The sacred mountain trembles,
> The bridge crumbles.
> Now the Master dwindles."

He wept. Then he said to Tze Kung, "For a long time the world has been in a dreadful state. No one would listen to me—indeed, they didn't know what I was talking about."

The old friends walked to and fro. Confucius said, "In Hsia, they place coffins on the east steps of the temple. In Chou, they place them on the west. In Yin, they place them between two pillars. Last night I dreamed I was between two pillars receiving the sacrificial offerings for the dead." He paused and added, "I suppose that dream means I am really a man of Yin!"

But the dream had a graver meaning, and he knew it.

He died seven days after. His last words were, "Will no ruler come forward and take me as his Master?"

Tze Kung led the mourning, and they buried him north of Ch'ü-fu on the riverbank.

The Years After

The high mountain, he looked toward it,
The distant road, he walked along it.

—Sse-Ma Ch'ien

When Confucius died, his disciples retired into huts built close to his grave, and they mourned him for three years, the length of time that sons mourn for fathers. Many of them held important posts and high offices of state; some of them were young men at the beginning of their careers. Yet, it is a fact that their names do not appear in the annals of those times for the few years after the Master went from them.

The huts were never really vacated. They became part of the family temple of Confucius that was built there. This temple became a shrine where, 350 years later, the Master's first biographer, Sse-Ma Ch'ien, saw his personal belongings, his vehicles, garments, and sacrificial vessels, lovingly preserved. In modern times it has been the site of the most important and richest of the Confucian temples where, under the old regime, scholars and mandarins and the emperor himself would come to offer reverence to the shade of their ancestor-of-state.

Yen Hui's prediction that people would take some time to understand the truths Confucius wished to teach them turned out to be correct. But through the growing fame of the *Lun Yü,* the *Collected Sayings,* and the dedicated apostleship of his pupils, including his brilliant grandson, Tze Sse, his ideas gained ground steadily, and two hundred years after his death, they came to glorious fruition in the teachings of Mencius (371–289 B.C.), a scholar and teacher who is said to have studied under a pupil of Tze Sse.

The teachings fell under a cloud in the next half-century. Their humanity aroused the enmity of Shih Huang-ti, the founder of the first Chinese empire. His dynasty, the Ch'in, was the one that gave China her name. The strict military state he established lasted for only fourteen years, but during this brief span hundreds of Confucian scholars were buried, burned, or boiled alive. The Confucian books were also burned—except the *I Ching,* which Shih Huang-ti needed in order to tell his fortune.

That fortune was ruin and an early death. The Han Dynasty which followed began a peaceful era during which Confucius took supreme rank among the masters of thought. Confucian scholars came out of hiding and began to reconstruct from memory the Confucian books. A descendant of Confucius produced some texts of the *Lun Yü,* the *Analects,* which he said he had found in the walls of the family temple.

In the course of time, the Confucians restored the old texts as best they could, and in the *Li Chi,* the *Book of Rites,* wrote down their Master's opinions. These became also the opinions of the Han emperors, and they remained the official opinions of state for more than two thousand years, until the revolution of 1912 brought the "Constitution of China"—as an instrument of power—to an end.

Bibliography

The life of Confucius, as it has been told in this book, is based largely on the *Lun Yü* and on the *Historical Record* of Sse-Ma Ch'ien, who was a court historian during the Han Dynasty. These works, particularly the *Lun Yü*, contain the earliest possible traditions and words of the Master that we can know. Quotations from the *Great Learning*, the *Doctrine of the Mean*, and the *Book of Filial Piety* are from the *Li Chi*, of which they are a part. This is a reconstructed work of the Han Dynasty.

All conversations not from the *Lun Yü* are from Richard Wilhelm's version of the *Historical Record*. In altering these texts in order to bring them closer to modern idiom, I have tried to be faithful to their meaning and spirit, preserving the Master's humorous manner.

Some modern books that have assisted me greatly are listed separately. Students who wish to pursue Confucius further should know that James Ware's recent translation of the *Lun Yü* is widely available in paperback; and that the biographical and historical works of H. G. Creel are as entertaining as scholarly books can be.

Chang, Chi-yun, *A Life of Confucius,* trans. by Shih Chao-yin. Taipei, China Culture Publishing Foundation, 1954.

H. G. Creel, *Chinese Thought from Confucius to Mao Tse-tung.* New York, New American Library, 1951.

H. G. Creel, *Confucius, the Man and the Myth.* New York, The John Day Company, 1949.

M. M. Dawson, *The Conduct of Life: the Basic Thoughts of Confucius.* New York, The Garden City Publishing Company, 1941.

Alfred Doeblin, *The Living Thoughts of Confucius.* New York, Longmans, Green and Company, 1940.

Shigeki Kaizuka, *Confucius,* trans. by Geoffrey Bownas. London, George Allen & Unwin Ltd., 1956.

Arthur Waley, *Three Ways of Thought in Ancient China.* Garden City, Doubleday and Company, n.d.

James R. Ware, *The Sayings of Confucius.* New York, New American Library, 1955.

Richard Wilhelm, *Confucius and Confucianism,* trans. by George H. Danton and Annina Periam Danton. New York, Harcourt, Brace and Company, 1931.

Index